Headline Series

No. 285   **FOREIGN POLICY ASSOCIATION** $4.00

The Shah, the Ayatollah, and the United States

by James A. Bill

	Introduction	3
1	**Prelude to Revolution**	9
2	**A Dynasty Ends and U.S. Policy Unravels**	21
3	**Rise and Fall of the Moderates**	35
4	**The Hostage Crisis**	49
5	**The Iran-Iraq War**	57
	Talking It Over	69
	Annotated Reading List	70

Cover Design: Ed Bohon

Sept./Oct. 1987
Published June 1988

18306316

9-89

The Author

JAMES A. BILL is professor of government and director of the Wendy and Emery Reves Center for International Studies at The College of William and Mary. A leading authority on the Middle East, he holds a Ph.D. from Princeton University and has observed the Iranian-American tragedy firsthand for over 25 years. His research took him to Iran during the height of the revolution. The author and editor of books on the Middle East, Dr. Bill has published articles in *Foreign Affairs, The Middle East Journal* and *Comparative Politics.* He has appeared on numerous national television programs, including CBS News specials on Iran and the MacNeil-Lehrer News Hour.

The Foreign Policy Association

The Foreign Policy Association is a private, nonprofit, nonpartisan educational organization. Its purpose is to stimulate wider interest and more effective participation in, and greater understanding of, world affairs among American citizens. Among its activities is the continuous publication, dating from 1935, of the HEADLINE SERIES. The author is responsible for factual accuracy and for the views expressed. FPA itself takes no position on issues of U.S. foreign policy.

HEADLINE SERIES (ISSN 0017-8780) is published five times a year, January, March, May, September and November, by the Foreign Policy Association, Inc., 729 Seventh Ave., New York, N.Y. 10019. Chairman, Robert V. Lindsay; President, John W. Kiermaier; Editor in Chief, Nancy L. Hoepli; Senior Editor, Ann R. Monjo; Associate Editor, K. M. Rohan. Subscription rates, $15.00 for 5 issues; $25.00 for 10 issues; $30.00 for 15 issues. Single copy price $4.00. Discount 25% on 10 to 99 copies; 30% on 100 to 499; 35% on 500 to 999; 40% on 1,000 or more. Payment must accompany orders for $8 or less. Add $1.50 for postage. Second-class postage paid at New York, N.Y. POSTMASTER: Send address changes to HEADLINE SERIES, Foreign Policy Association, 729 Seventh Ave., New York, N.Y. 10019. Copyright 1988 by Foreign Policy Association, Inc. Composed and printed at Science Press, Ephrata, Pennsylvania.

Library of Congress Catalog Card No. 88-70867
ISBN 0-87124-120-X

Introduction

Early on the morning of Sunday, May 25, 1986, six men boarded a black Boeing 707 aircraft in Tel Aviv, Israel. They were bound for Tehran, capital of the Islamic Republic of Iran. The six men, a team whose mission had been approved by President Ronald Reagan himself, carried with them a chocolate cake prepared in a kosher bakery in Tel Aviv, six Blackhawk .357 Magnum pistols in presentation boxes, and one pallet of spare parts for Iran's Hawk missiles. Their mission was to exchange the badly needed spare parts for four Americans being held hostage in Lebanon. When they landed in Tehran an hour and a half ahead of schedule that morning, they found themselves immediately embroiled in controversy and tense diplomatic conflict.

Editor's note: This HEADLINE SERIES *is excerpted from James A. Bill's* The Eagle and the Lion: The Tragedy of American-Iranian Relations, *published by Yale University Press in April 1988. (Copyright © 1988 by James A Bill.) This adaptation from the 520-page original was made with the cooperation of the author.*

Carrying Irish passports, the six official adventurers included former head of the National Security Council staff Robert "Bud" McFarlane, Lt. Col. Oliver North, NSC official Howard Teicher, Central Intelligence Agency (CIA) Iran specialist George Cave, a communications expert, and Amiram Nir, an Israeli confidant of Prime Minister Shimon Peres.

When the six left Tehran three days later, the pallet of arms remained in Iran. The four American hostages remained in Lebanon. United States-Iranian tensions had deepened, not relaxed. A secret, risky mission that Colonel North had expected to go "peachy keen" had failed ignominiously. Yet it was on the return trip to the United States that North confided to McFarlane that the escapade had not been a "total lost cause," since funds received from the Iranians for arms had been applied to Central America.

The Iranian-U.S. arms affair capped a long period of confused and confusing U.S. policy toward an ancient Middle Eastern country of great strategic significance in the international community of nations. It demonstrated forcibly that American foreign policy toward postrevolutionary Iran reflected many of the flaws that had dominated U.S. policy before the revolution: flaws of massive ignorance, bureaucratic conflict, Sovietcentricity, military obsessions, and the prevalence of informal or privatized decisionmaking all transcended the revolution as America carried past mistakes into the future.

Informed Iranians often wrote and spoke about America's lack of knowledge of their country. They murmured quietly about the naïveté of Americans. On the other hand, these same Iranians insisted that the United States was intimately acquainted with everything that transpired in their country. In the Iranian view, the CIA was omnipresent in Iran; what Americans did not know for themselves, they found out through their connections with the omniscient British or the stealthy Israelis.

In the United States itself, leading policymakers through the years were consistently confident that they knew Iran very well indeed. This confidence was shared in varying degree by every U.S. President from Eisenhower through Reagan.

A Century of Goodwill

Few international relationships have had a more positive beginning than that which characterized Iranian-American contacts for more than a century. The United States stood aloof from the great-power rivalry of Britain and Russia over Iranian territory. For decades, Iran managed to maintain its independence as a nation-state by playing the two great powers against one another. Whenever the two rivals came to an understanding, Iranian leaders saw their country's independence and identity in serious jeopardy. Such was the case, for example, in 1907, when the two powers signed the Anglo-Russian Agreement, effectively dividing Iran into zones of influence. The Russians were dominant in the north, the British in the southeast, and there was a neutral zone in between.

Even more dangerous to Iranian independence was the scenario in which either great power gained clear ascendancy over the other. This occurred in 1825–28 when a Persian-Russian war resulted in a treaty that not only cost Iran all of its territory west of the Caspian Sea but also forced it to grant extraterritorial privileges to Russian citizens resident in Iran. Another example was the Reuter Concession of 1872, which granted a British subject a monopoly over virtually all of Iran's economic and financial resources. As Lord Curzon stated, it was "the most complete and extraordinary surrender of the entire industrial resources of a kingdom into foreign hands that has probably ever been dreamed of." Another case in point was the Anglo-Persian Agreement of 1919, which was concluded in secret and which gave Britain enormous political, military and economic control over Iran. Although these last two agreements were ultimately rejected, they stood as stark reminders of the external threats to Iran's independence.

As Iran zigged and zagged its way through a political thicket inhabited by such interested and predatory creatures as Russia and Britain, its leaders constantly looked for third forces to exercise a neutralizing influence. Along with Germany and, to a lesser extent, France, the United States represented a major hope in this respect. Until 1953, American statements and activities convinced Iran's leaders that this hope was well placed. As early as 1919, for example, the United States had strongly protested to Britain about its secret agreement of that year. And in the mid-1940s, the United States took the forward position in pressing the Soviet Union to withdraw its forces from Azerbaijan. They withdrew in April 1946. For motives both national and personal, Iranian political leaders sought "to use America as a political balancer and an economic Santa Claus." Partially because the United States played this role quite well, Americans were greatly admired in Iran.

After its part in the 1953 overthrow of popular Prime Minister Muhammad Musaddiq, who had nationalized Iranian oil, the United States found itself the object of growing Iranian criticism. Both the moderate, nationalistic opposition forces as well as the more radical voices on the left began to refer to the United States as an imperialistic, oppressive external force. At the same time, the Shi'i religious leaders began to condemn America and American policy. Iranians of all political persuasions increasingly developed a negative image of the United States. They no longer saw America as an external, liberating force whose influence would protect Iran from its traditional enemies, Britain and Russia. Instead, they developed a perspective in which the protector had become the exploiter. In the view of many Iranians, the first significant move in the American turnabout occurred with the fall of the Musaddiq movement. Here, according to Iranian nationalists, the United States chose to ally itself with the imperial interests of Britain and in the process rescued Shah Mohammad Reza Pahlavi, a man who had fled ignominiously from his own country. As Britain retreated from its preeminent role in the Persian Gulf, the United States replaced it as the new, obtrusive and interventionist external power.

Throughout the 1970s the United States increased its influence in Iran to levels reminiscent of the direct interventions of Britain and Russia during the heyday of colonialism. The traditional Persian paranoia and accompanying resentment were increasingly transferred from Britain and the U.S.S.R. to the United States, especially as America entwined itself more and more with

**Before the revolution: President Jimmy Carter offers a toast
to the shah of Iran.**

the governing regime in Iran. By the time of the Iranian
revolution in 1978, America's reservoir of historical goodwill had
been drained dry. The violent, antimonarchical movement had a
sharp anti-American edge that became even sharper in reaction to
policies developed in Washington in response to the revolution. In
the years following the revolution, Iranian-American relations
reached an all-time low. When the Carter Administration admitted the shah to the United States for medical treatment on October
22, 1979, a group of extremist Iranian students took over the
American embassy in Tehran and held over 50 U.S. citizens
hostage for almost 15 months. During this time the two countries
engaged in practically every form of conflict short of all-out war.

What happened? How could two allies and longtime friends
reach such a state of estrangement that their confrontation had
come to harm seriously the national interests of both parties?
What forces at work in Iran, the United States, and the world
contributed to this conflict? Can damaged Iranian-American

relations be repaired? What does the future hold for these relations—relations that are of great significance to both countries?

Profile of a Regional Power

Iran is a country of 50 million people, a number almost twice that of all the other Persian Gulf countries put together. Sharing a 1,600-mile border with the Soviet Union in the north and fronting the important Strait of Hormuz to the south, Iran is a nation of special geostrategic significance. Iran has 10 percent of the world's proven reserves of petroleum (about 65 billion barrels), and throughout the 1970s Iran was the world's second largest oil exporter. It also possesses the world's second largest reserves of natural gas. Conservatively estimated at 500 trillion cubic feet, these reserves are the energy equivalent of another 82 billion barrels of oil. In these circumstances, the state of Iranian-American relations assumes a special importance to every American. Is there any relationship acceptable to the peoples and governments of both countries?

What general policy lessons does the tragic history of Iranian-American relations teach? As a case study in U.S. foreign policy, what might this history indicate about the strengths and weaknesses of such policymaking? How might it affect American relations with other Middle Eastern and Third World countries? What does it indicate about the future of the United States in a world caught in the midst of revolutionary change? Can we avoid similar imbroglios elsewhere as we navigate ourselves through stormy international waters toward the year 2000? These are among the questions I will seek to answer in this HEADLINE SERIES.

1

Prelude to Revolution

Two years into his presidency, Jimmy Carter watched in helpless disbelief as Iran exploded in revolution and one of America's major political allies in the shifting terrain of the Middle East collapsed like a pillar of sand. On January 16, 1979, the shah himself, with a few members of his family and inner circle, fled his country for the final time. Ayatollah Ruhollah Khomeini, the stern, charismatic leader and inspiration of the revolution, arrived in Tehran from his Paris exile on February 1. And from February 9 to 11, the last remnants of the shah's once proud and loyal army fought their last stand at Dushan Tappah Air Force Base in east Tehran; a contingent of the Royal Guards, the Immortals, were crushed in a confrontation with rebelling air force cadets assisted by thousands of civilian guerrillas. American officials considered the fall of the Pahlavi dynasty a foreign policy catastrophe of tremendous proportion.

The year 1977 set the stage for the revolution. These critical 12 months contained, in retrospect, all the signs of imminent political collapse. Although few read these signs, they were visible in the economic system, which was in the midst of a sharp retrenchment; in the religious revival, where hundreds of thousands of Iranians returned to the fundamentals of Shi'i activism; and in the political realm, where the Pahlavi regime attempted to cope with growing dissent in an inconsistent and ineffective manner.

The phenomenal economic growth rate of 1973–75 came to a sudden halt as oil revenues leveled off between 1975 and 1978. This "superboom," in which the economy had veered "virtually out of conventional control," had brought about Iranian plans to create a herd of economic white elephants that included turbo trains, nuclear power plants, heart transplant centers, and a multibillion dollar naval base at Chah Bahar on the Indian Ocean. Meanwhile, by 1977, the agricultural growth rate had stagnated to less than 3 percent, and rural-urban migration had shifted into a pattern of all-out flight. At the same time, a huge rural-urban income distribution gap became visible; careful observers indicated that this gap had tripled since the mid-1960s. Government studies documented the severe shortage of skilled laborers, who were replaced by a foreign work force that numbered over 300,000 and included Indian and Pakistani physicians, Filipino nurses, Korean truck drivers, U.S. military and industrial advisers, and Afghan laborers. While bad weather and migration had cut wheat, rice, and barley production in the country, the peasants lacked incentive to grow grains since they could not compete with imports that were being sold at subsidized prices. Meanwhile, the situation in the cities was aggravated by a severe recession in the construction industry.

Although the economy cooled off and a serious retrenchment policy took hold, the runaway corruption that had accompanied the boom showed little sign of abating. The enormity and visibility of this corruption, which involved huge bribes, fraudulent land schemes and extravagant commissions on contracts, hurt the country both economically and politically. As the creeping corruption accelerated into a mad dash for instant wealth, the shah's family and close associates ran at the head of the pack.

In an attempt to cool the overheated economy, the regime inaugurated a heavy-handed anti-inflation policy that involved sending groups of zealous young inspectors through the bazaars seeking price gougers. This policy wreaked havoc in the traditional business community; many of its leaders were arrested, exiled, and punished in a variety of ways. The arbitrary nature of this action alienated the bazaar, the heart of the Iranian economy. As part of this drastic austerity campaign, the regime terminated its subsidies to the Shi'i religious establishment, further alienating the already aggrieved *ulama* (Muslim clerics).

The technocracy, Western-educated and enormously confi-dent, brushed aside the criti-cisms of informed observers who warned of the great fragility of

UPI/Bettmann Newsphotos

Ayatollah Ruhollah Khomeini

the economic system. In 1975, for example, internationally known petroleum analyst Walter Levy had warned the Iranian technocrats that they had overextended themselves, that they had substituted "black gold," which was in fact "manna from heav-en," for any fundamental, lasting economic system. Bright, enthusiastic, and ambitious young planners responded glibly and confidently using technocratic jargon they had learned in Western universities. In fact, rhetoric and jargon substituted for meaning-ful action and effective policy.

This was a time of conferences, seminars, and long discussions about "infrastructures" and "bottlenecks." First used by the technocrats, these terms soon found their way into the vocabulary of the shah himself. Once the shah began speaking about the need for a *zirbana* (infrastructure) in order to alleviate the *tangna* (bottlenecks), then every planner increased his own use of these terms. Although several economic problems existed, many of the bottlenecks were social and political in nature as the lack of effective nationwide political institutions increased disaffection among the Iranian masses, many of whom now returned to the fundamentals of Islam.

The Turn to Islam

Throughout 1977 thousands of young Iranians continued turning to Islam as a force of liberation and a refuge from the oppressive politics of Pahlavi rule. This revival, unprecedented in recent Iranian history, was most visible in secondary schools and universities, where large numbers of young women reveiled themselves and attended classes completely clad in black *chadurs*. At Isfahan University in August 1977, one young lady in a chadur explained very simply why she had returned to the veil: "I am making a statement."

Men and women flocked to religious study centers, where they discussed social and political matters in terms of the lives of the infallible religious leaders (*Imams*) of Shi'i Islam. The explosive strength of this religious revival was seen at Tehran University on October 9, 1977, when two dozen masked students, demanding the segregation of women on campus, went on a rampage, smashing windows and burning buses. That fall also saw numerous religious demonstrations in the holy city of Qum.

Although American diplomats admitted their lack of knowledge about this religious resurgence and instead focused on opposition from the secular left, they could not help but sense that some kind of religious force was gathering in Iran.

Politically, 1977 was the year in which the shah and his political elite announced dramatic plans to implement a new policy. The key phrase used to describe this new political program was "the year of liberalization." The core of this "liberalization" program was called *musharikat* (participation). Like the economic buzzwords bottlenecks and infrastructures, the new political vocabulary did not necessarily indicate a fundamental change in political reality.

Despite the conventional argument that the shah began to liberalize his political system solely in response to Carter's human rights policy, the reasons for the liberalization, which in fact began months before Carter became President, were far more complex. The shah chose to modify dramatically his policy of control for five reasons.

First, the shah was shrewd enough to recognize that the

repressive policy of the previous five years had been counterproductive. The evident commitment of the young guerrillas to their cause and their increasingly suicidal missions troubled him. Furthermore, close security advisers such as Gen. Hussein Fardust, who opposed the ruthless, crude techniques of Col. Nimatullah Nassiri, the head of the shah's notorious secret police, SAVAK, reportedly convinced the shah to take matters again into his own hands and to lighten his political touch.

Second, during these few years the shah began to consider seriously the long-term future of his dynasty. He was particularly concerned about the accession to power of his eldest son, 16-year-old Crown Prince Reza. At this time he was also well aware that he had cancer, the disease having been diagnosed by French physicians a few years earlier. He wanted a strategy that would maximize the chances for his son to succeed him without incident. He also wondered privately about the method of governance that would be most congenial to his son. As American officials judged it, the shah had come to believe that a more liberal, open style might be the best for the future and for his son.

Third, the repressive tactics had been gaining increased international attention. Both the terrorist acts that occurred in the streets of Tehran and the growing chorus of world criticism troubled the shah. He sought favorable international mass media coverage for his country and especially for himself.

Fourth, having jettisoned a number of his older advisers, the shah in 1976–77 brought in a number of bright young technocrats of more liberal disposition. Many were former opponents of Pahlavi rule and had associations with Musaddiq's National Front. During these years Empress Farah also assumed more political influence, and her circle consisted of young professionals who counseled political reform.

Last and least, the shah's commitment to liberalization was reinforced by the election of Carter to the presidency of the United States. The shah was betting on his friend Gerald R. Ford to win the election and was clearly upset when the Democrat Carter was elected. He immediately sent two of his best "America watchers" to Washington to gather information about Carter, a little-known figure to the Iranian political elite. The shah feared that Carter might prove to be another John F. Kennedy, whom he had disliked immensely, partly for reasons of personal envy and partly for the pressure that Kennedy had put on him to reform his political system. In the end, the shah determined to see for himself and arranged a meeting with the new American President late in 1977. Meanwhile, he moved to deflect any possible criticism of his rule by publicizing the liberalization policy that he had initiated earlier in 1976.

The shah's liberalization policy was multipronged. He stressed the success of his White Revolution, a reform program he instituted that focused on such target areas as land reform and literacy. American officials were particularly fond of citing these measures when they testified before congressional committees investigating human rights violations in Iran. Rather than confront the issue of such violations, they recited the progress made by the shah's White Revolution. The details of this reform program, many of which were quite accurate and did indeed represent certain material advances and economic growth, seldom failed to impress American audiences.

A second tactic, resuscitated and expanded in 1976–77, was the emphasis on a party system that promoted a variant of democracy in Iran. In this case, it was the single Rastakhiz party, which the shah had created in 1975. Government spokesmen stressed that this party enabled everyone to participate in the political process. When the question of forced membership in a single party was raised, they responded that there were in fact two wings to the party. Pahlavi ideologues thus argued that Iran had the best of both worlds, a one-party system and a two-party system all rolled into one!

'Loosening the Reigns a Little'

Besides the continuing reference to the White Revolution and the mass political party, the shah's government in 1977 introduced a number of other policies that highlighted the attempt to ease the social and political pressures that had been building in the system. These included several highly publicized and selective releases of political prisoners, a loosening of the tight system of censorship, and the establishment of various study groups to hear the complaints and grievances of the people. Furthermore, during the first 10 months of 1977, the regime invited three major international human rights groups—the International Red Cross, Amnesty International, and the International Commission of Jurists (ICJ)—into the country for a firsthand examination of social and political conditions. Although the efforts of Amnesty International received most world attention, the activities of the ICJ were especially effective since the shah took its recommendations most seriously.

Along with these policy changes, the shah shuffled the membership of his political elite. On August 6, 1977, he relieved Amir Abbas Hoveyda from his longtime position as prime minister and named him minister of court. The next day he appointed Jamshid Amuzegar as prime minister. Amuzegar's cabinet included 10 new faces, all educated technocrats. The new prime minister was above all else a technocrat who consciously avoided addressing basic political issues. Yet it was precisely the political situation that was the critical issue of the day.

The liberalization process struck a responsive chord in Iran. As the regime slowly lifted its lid on society, pent-up political pressures escaped immediately and explosively. When the newspaper *Kayhan* asked "What is wrong with Iran?" it received over 40,000 letters in response. It is important to note that during this period of relative liberalization, there was little violence in the streets. The nation and the guerrilla leaders were watching and waiting to see how serious the reforms would be. Their verdict was negative. The liberalization was partial; the reforms were superficial; the political system was to remain basically the same.

In fact, the shah pursued an inconsistent policy. While stressing liberalization and, in the shah's words as reported in an Iranian newspaper, attempting to "loosen the reigns [*sic*] a little," he at the same time argued for maintaining a strong centralized regime with his own role preeminent and predominant. The shah viewed opponents and dissidents as either "red" or "black"— Communists or reactionary clerics. Those Iranians who did not support the Rastakhiz party were "suffering from mental imbalance." A strong monarchy was essential in Iran, where no other kind of political system would work. Western societies suffered from a severe lack of social discipline, sloth and indolence and, as permissive societies, were destroying themselves. The Iranian monarchy was on the way to becoming the major political model for the world.

That the shah introduced his policy of liberalization arbitrarily from above convinced many Iranians that it was clearly a palliative developed to buy the regime more time while satisfying the new Democratic Administration in Washington. In the eyes of most, despite all the verbiage, the shah had opened the political door slightly, had sought to hold it there, and, when necessary, had instructed his police to slam it shut again.

The Carter Administration determined from the beginning that it would continue past American policies toward Iran, with a special sensitivity to the importance of that country as a major military force for stability in the Persian Gulf and as an influential force in the pricing of petroleum. America's special strategic relationship with Iran was to be protected at all costs. At the same time, the new Democratic Administration concluded that it would promote human rights policies in the international arena. In his inaugural address on January 20, 1977, President Carter had stated: "Our moral sense dictates a clear preference for those societies which share with us an abiding respect for individual human rights." An emphasis on human rights, it was argued, would be in the American national interest since it was both morally right and politically expedient. The Administration argued that American allies in Third World societies would in fact strengthen themselves politically by the promotion of human rights policies. One important part of the emphasis on human rights was a careful reexamination of American arms sales. Iran accounted for over half of all American arms sales.

Iran was centrally important to the fledgling Carter Administration. Carter's foreign policy team of Secretary of State Cyrus R. Vance and national security adviser Zbigniew Brzezinski were well aware that the shah's policies directly benefited the United

States. Vance himself listed five such positive policies: (1) the shah provided important economic assistance to countries in the area; (2) he helped reduce tensions in southwest Asia; (3) his forces had helped to defeat an insurgency in Oman; (4) he was "a reliable supplier of oil to the West"; he had, in fact, refused to join the 1973 Arab oil embargo; and (5) he was Israel's primary source of oil. Thus, "we decided early on that it was in our national interest to support the shah so he could continue to play a constructive role in regional affairs." Although human rights were a genuine concern for Carter, this issue was certainly not to take precedence over security and economic issues.

The Shah: Sizing up Carter

The shah was nervous about Carter's presidency, not only because of the general issue of human rights but also because of his own close past associations with the Nixon-Ford-Kissinger group. Ford had been a friendly and malleable political ally. Carter was an unknown. Furthermore, the shah's old friend Richard M. Helms had departed as U.S. ambassador to Iran in December 1976 and was not replaced until June 1977 by William H. Sullivan. The absence of a U.S. ambassador in Tehran during these critical months troubled the shah, who was busily trying to read every little sign out of Washington. The shah therefore determined to meet the new Democratic President as soon as possible in order to size him up and to make certain that he could count on the unwavering support of the United States for his regime. He thus began a quiet lobbying campaign for an exchange of official visits.

In May 1977, Secretary of State Vance traveled to Tehran, where he held important meetings with the shah. During a two-hour meeting on May 13 at Niavaran Palace, Vance invited the shah to Washington in November, informed him that the United States had decided to go ahead with the pending sale of 160 F-16 aircraft, promised that the President would seek congressional approval for the shah's request for the sophisticated airborne warning and control system (AWACS), and explained America's plans for convening a Geneva peace conference focusing on the Arab-Israeli dispute. In general terms he also indicated that the United States supported principles of human rights and praised the shah's recent policies of liberalization. The shah gave Vance a pointed lesson in the significance of human rights through 2,500 years of Iranian history and indicated that he had no trouble with America's emphasis on human rights as a general principle—as long as this policy was not directed at Iran and did not threaten Iran's security.

When Vance left Tehran, the shah was somewhat more confident about his capacity to deal politically with the Carter Administration. Vance had been appropriately impressed by the policy of liberalization begun a year before; he had promised to deliver the F-16s; he had even indicated Carter's willingness to support the controversial AWACS request. But while the shah had one interpretation of the Vance visit, the gathering opposition held quite another view.

The Opposition: A Case of Wishful Thinking

After Vance's visit, the word spread quickly through the extensive Iranian grapevine that the shah had just been given his orders from Washington: either liberalize or be removed. This fanciful interpretation of the Vance visit, based on a heavy portion of wishful thinking on the part of the opposition intelligentsia, was repeated until it soon became accepted fact in Tehran. The gap between what Vance had in fact said and what the growing Iranian opposition groups said he had said carried severe political consequences. The shah interpreted the visit as an important preliminary sign of Carter's support for his policies and autonomy. He now became somewhat less concerned about liberalization, and his police began again to take sporadic harsh actions against suspected opposition groups. The opposition, on the other hand, concluded that they could now operate under an American umbrella that had been raised by Vance. When this protective umbrella failed to appear and the shah's police cracked down, the political situation in Iran began to deteriorate rapidly.

Although the Carter Administration did not put any serious human rights pressure on the shah, the support of Carter's government for human rights more generally made it easy for the Iranian opposition, with its exaggerated belief in American influence over the shah, to conclude that the shah had been given his human rights marching orders. When the shah cracked down, the opposition forces, in line with their obsession with foreign influence, drew the reverse conclusion—the United States had now ordered the shah to reestablish a policy of repression.

Throughout the summer and early fall of 1977, President Carter sent numerous signals of support to the shah. The most important example was the Administration's campaign to sell the shah the technologically advanced $1.2 billion AWACS. Despite his public determination to reduce American arms sales across the board, early in 1977 Carter chose to make Iran an exception. In so doing, he suddenly ran into surprising opposition from a number of influential senators and representatives who questioned the wisdom of this policy.

Senator Thomas Eagleton (D-Mo.) stated that "this is not an ordinary arms deal. It was born in the atmosphere of secret deals of prior Administrations. . . . It violates the tenets of restraints in the arms sales policies which are being developed by the new Carter Administration." He went on to specify presciently the particular problems, which he outlined as an increased American presence in Iran and a serious security risk since Iran's government, "centered on a mortal leader, is fragile and subject to radical change. To endorse this sale is to take an imprudent risk to American national security." Through the good offices of Senator Hubert H. Humphrey (D-Minn.), a compromise was worked out that ultimately resulted in the approval of the sale in the fall.

Meanwhile, the Carter Administration, so publicly committed to slowing arms sales, also approved the $1.8 billion sale of an additional 160 General Dynamics F-16 fighters to Iran and immediately began considering a further Pahlavi request for 140 more F-16s.

In sum, early in the Carter Administration the shah had effectively convinced the new President that the Pahlavi regime was exceptionally important to the United States. And the United States reacted accordingly. The issue of human rights did not figure heavily in the political equation; it was far down on Carter's list of issues concerning the United States and Iran.

On November 15, 1977, while Jimmy and Rosalynn Carter and the shah and empress of Iran stood on the White House lawn in a welcoming ceremony, thousands of shouting students were demonstrating just outside the gates. The police resorted to tear gas in an attempt to control the demonstrators, but uncooperative breezes carried the gases directly into the faces of the presidential party. With tears running down their faces, the Carters and Pahlavis cut the formalities and pleasantries short, but they never forgot this embarrassing event. President Carter later referred to this incident as an "augury"; it had created "the semblance of grief," and almost two years later "there would be real grief in our country because of Iran." The demonstrations in Washington were paralleled by similar demonstrations in Tehran against the shah and his American supporters. These public events should have alerted the world to the seriousness of the situation in Iran, whose political system would soon begin to unravel.

The November 15–16, 1977, meetings paralleled those the shah had had with past Presidents. In fact, Carter's behavior and decisions concerning Iran were not unlike those of Lyndon B. Johnson, Richard M. Nixon and Ford, all of whom the shah considered very special friends. There was a brief private chat between the two heads of state about the general issue of human rights, but the monarch firmly pointed out that Iran's laws had to be enforced and that these laws were designed to combat communism, which was the real threat to his country.

The major issues actually discussed during the Washington visit were oil prices, arms purchases, nuclear power plants, the Arab-Israeli conflict, and Soviet influence in Somalia and Ethiopia. In general, the shah agreed to assume a moderating posture on the issue of petroleum prices and offered to assist in persuading his friends, King Hussein of Jordan and President Anwar al-Sadat of Egypt, to follow the American lead in working for a Middle East peace settlement.

2

A Dynasty Ends
and U.S. Policy Unravels

Iran under the great leadership of the shah is an island of stability in one of the more troubled areas of the world. This is a great tribute to you, Your Majesty, and to your leadership, and to the respect, admiration and love which your people give to you.
—President Jimmy Carter, Tehran, December 31, 1977

In order to acquire name and fame, Ruhollah Khomeini became a tool for the red and black colonialists who have sought to discredit the revolution of the shah and the people. . . . Actually, Khomeini is known as the Indian Sayyid (Sayyid Hindi). . . . He lived in India for a time where he was in touch with British colonial circles and it is said that when young he composed love poems under the pen name of Hindi.
—Ittila'at, Tehran, January 7, 1978

These two ill-conceived statements, both presented within one fateful week, helped light the fuse that led directly to the revolutionary explosion that was to tear Iran apart over the next 14 months. Carter's unquestioning support for the shah signaled to the Pahlavi regime that it could continue to pursue its policy of alternating reform and repression. Pahlavi functionaries immediately adopted a new aggressive strategy. They underestimated the depth and intensity of the opposition, which was seething after Carter's unfortunate visit. The major tactical error was a direct, vicious personal attack on Khomeini in an article entitled "Iran and Red and Black Colonialism" published in the newspaper *Ittila'at* on January 7, 1978. Cleverly picking up the shah's old argument about the foreign-inspired attacks on his modern and progressive ideas by red leftist intellectuals on the one hand and black religious reactionaries on the other, the writer carelessly put Khomeini's finger on this double-barreled political shotgun. He then assailed Khomeini's character directly, accusing him of being a foreigner, a writer of love sonnets, an opponent of the shah's great reform program, a tool of the British, and responsible for the deaths of many Iranians in the June 1963 riots.

The day after the newspaper attack on Khomeini, January 8, the clerics and religious students in the holy city of Qum staged massive demonstrations and protest marches. With the American President back in Washington after his enthusiastic embrace of the shah, the government was scarcely restrained by concerns of liberalization and human rights. The police opened fire on the crowds in Qum, killing two dozen people and wounding many more. Religious leaders were among those killed. This event set off a long series of demonstrations and violent incidents throughout Iran that gained momentum with time. The protest marches grew in size and spread in number as the year passed. The shah's police and military forces responded forcefully, but their bullets ultimately only stitched together the fragmented protesting organizations until the bloodstained patchwork quilt of opposition forces covered the entire nation.

The violent events of 1978–79 have been chronicled in great detail. From January 1978 to February 1979 not a month passed without major antiregime demonstrations. The opposition and violence spiraled as the traditional Shi'i 40-day period of mourning brought further opportunities for demonstrations and killings. The death of one family member radicalized other relatives, who then joined the active opposition; this extended-family phenomenon added to the cumulative nature of the revolution.

Although a number of influential observers have argued repeatedly both that the shah lost his will to control the situation and that he did so partly because he was ill and partly because he was concerned about pressure from President Carter, this position fails the test of historical fact. Surrounded by trusted hard-line military advisers, the shah initially gave orders to put down the disturbances with as much force as necessary. The bloodshed in Tabriz in February, Tehran in September, Isfahan in December, and Mashhad in early January 1979 bears witness to this tough policy. During these bloody months, troops fired on funeral processions, invaded homes of religious leaders, and, on a number of documented occasions, fired directly into unarmed crowds of men, women and children.

Careful research indicates that an estimated 10,000 to 12,000 persons were killed and another 45,000 to 50,000 injured during the 14-month revolutionary upheaval. Whatever the exact number, it is indisputable that the casualties far exceeded those of any previous political crisis in modern Iranian history. The ultimate futility of trying to put down in blood a revolt by millions became clear to the shah himself before it did to a number of U.S. officials who even now, a decade after the revolution, continue to perpetuate the myth that more force and more deaths could have salvaged the Pahlavi regime. In late fall 1978, the shah came to the conclusion that he would not and could not rule a country in which he had to stand in the flowing blood of his people. In short, he understood that he could not militarily occupy his own country.

Portrait of an Ayatollah

Through 1978 the opposition solidified under the hammer blows of Pahlavi police and military forces. Meanwhile, the guiding inspiration of the revolution, Ayatollah Khomeini, kept the pressure on, pushing relentlessly to end the Pahlavi dynasty. From the holy Shi'i city of Najaf, in Iraq, until October 6, and then from a small home near Paris, Khomeini directed the burgeoning opposition movement. He did so through an extensive personal network, the nodes of which were a large number of key religious and bazaari followers. It is reliably estimated that over the years Khomeini helped educate hundreds of *mujtahids* (high-ranking, learned clerics with the capacity to "interpret") and that during his last years at Qum over 1,200 students (*shagirdan*) had taken courses from him. The Khomeini network had been in place ever since his exile 14 years earlier, and over the years it had absorbed and then distributed millions upon millions of dollars among the ayatollah's followers and the impoverished masses who were his constituents. The Khomeini network was also used as a flexible communications grid to transmit constantly his ideas and teachings. When the revolutionary sparks ignited, this network was firmly in place and served as an extremely effective organizational medium for the movement.

Ayatollah Ruhollah Khomeini was born on September 24, 1902, in a small town approximately 60 miles from Tehran. He studied for many years in Arak and then in Qum under the guidance of some of the leading religious Shi'i scholars of the day. A follower of the very learned, if apolitical, Shi'i grand ayatollah, Sayyid Muhammad Hussein Burujirdi, Khomeini nurtured strong feelings about the Pahlavi political system, which he considered illegitimate, corrupt and repressive. It was after the death of Burujirdi in March 1961 that Khomeini began his career as political activist.

Protest, Prison and Exile

Khomeini's first serious public protests against the government occurred late in 1962 when he opposed the repeal of the requirement that local assembly officials be male Muslims. His active public political career, therefore, began when he was 60 years of age. In 1963 he stepped up his opposition by challenging aspects of the shah's White Revolution. This led to his arrest in June and helped precipitate the 1963 national uprising. He was released from prison and again confronted the system in October 1964 over the American-supported status of forces agreement. This in turn led to his expulsion and exile. Khomeini's 30 months of confrontational politics then gave way to an extended period of lower-key, persistent opposition from exile in Iraq. The 30-month spurt of political activity had given him the image of a fearless, uncompromising champion of the oppressed, and he became a Shi'i folk hero who was both persecuted and powerful.

Whether he is judged a man of unshaking morality and principle or one of vindictive religious-lined tunnel vision, there can be no doubt that Khomeini pursued his goals with single-minded determination and total dedication. From the early 1960s onward, he sought the destruction of the Pahlavi dynasty, which he felt had sold Iran's soul to the West while promoting corruption, immorality, and oppression in Iran.

Throughout 1978, Khomeini issued proclamations from Najaf condemning the shah, praising Islam, castigating the United States for its support of the shah, and honoring those Iranians who were demonstrating and rebelling against Pahlavi rule. His speeches were emotional and politically astute. He spoke the language of the Iranian masses and sensitively highlighted their everyday problems and suffering. And he did so through the idiom of religion. He spoke as a radical religious populist. He constantly encouraged the people of Iran to challenge the ruling class, not to "swallow the poison the holders of authority wish to force down our throats." He exhorted them to die if necessary in their resistance, "to water the roots of the tree of Islam with their blood." And he cleverly turned the tables on the regime by arguing that "the shah and his government are in a state of armed rebellion against the justice-seeking people of Iran, against the constitution, and against the liberating decrees of Islam." In the words of Khomeini and his growing mass constituency, the shah was a rebel against both his own people and his own religion. This rebellious regime had to be overthrown at any cost.

As Iranians increasingly rallied to the cries of Khomeini and as the government's hard-line tactics yielded counterproductive results, the shah desperately attempted to resort again to proven political moves. He continually shuffled the deck of political actors close to him, arbitrarily discarding those he considered dispensable and retaining others. These personality shifts were too little, too late. As the shah's last ambassador to the United Nations stated, "So, where immediate surgery was required, the shah used first aid." Like the entire liberalization program, these changes were half-hearted and poorly implemented.

Jalah Square: A Revolution Builds

I lived for two weeks in November-December 1978 among the masses of people in southeast Tehran on a small alley behind a gas station near Jalah Square, where the Black Friday massacres of antiregime demonstrators had taken place earlier. Here large crowds waited in line for their kerosene and rationed meat, and shouted slogans against the shah. Taxi drivers spit in the direction of the shah's soldiers, and students combed the city for pictures of the royal family to tear down and deface. Luxury hotels, cinemas, and liquor stores stood silently as dark, windowless, bombed-out hulks. Anti-Americanism was intense, and a wild, powerful sentiment pervaded the crowded sidewalks, markets and streets. This was the heartbeat of the revolution, and the people's anger swelled out of south Tehran. Young bearded representatives of Aqa (as they then referred to Khomeini) hurried constantly to the key homes and mosques where they organized the opposition and dispensed Aqa's latest directives.

Meanwhile, 20 miles to the north, in Niavaran Palace, an unreal, eerie atmosphere prevailed. The shah sat silently at his desk, while Empress Farah nervously greeted guests from whom she earnestly, almost desperately, sought advice. As the shah sat stunned and suspicious, even Farah was unable to get him to follow her advice. In her words, "the husband does not always listen to the wife." But both resisted the fact that this time the masses were laying full blame for their plight at the feet of the Pahlavis—and those who backed the royal family. The cultural and political distance between Jalah Square in southeast Tehran and Niavaran Palace to the north was much greater than the geographic reality. Meanwhile, the growing clouds of revolutionary anger, containing the thundering shouts of the huge crowds, slowly and inexorably encompassed the shah and his diminishing group of loyal followers.

The shah's grip slipped in the face of increasing turbulence and the flight of many of the leading members of the Pahlavi elite. Those who met with the shah at the end of 1978 reported that he seemed listless, depressed, baffled and shaken. Some have concluded that if he had acted with firmness and resolution, he could have faced down the revolution. They have attributed his indecision to a number of factors, blaming everyone and everything from Carter to the shah's cancer. But the fact is that times had changed. The shah's early mistakes had been institutionalized over the years. In late 1978, he stood in the path of millions of

Iranian citizens in revolt against him. He did take actions, both forceful and accommodating. Nothing worked. It is no wonder that his grip weakened and his mind wavered.

On January 16, 1979, the shah and empress of Iran and a small entourage boarded a silver-and-blue Boeing 707 for Egypt. As the shah flew out of the country for the final time, masses of people rushed to the streets of the major cities and held frenzied celebrations. On February 1, Ayatollah Ruhollah Khomeini arrived in Tehran from France, and the Iranian revolution became a reality. The United States, a country that had confidently rested its vital interests in the Middle East on the Pahlavi pillar, watched in shock and alarm as the pillar collapsed with a roar heard round the world.

The United States in the Iranian Revolution

The American foreign policy establishment was badly divided over the Iranian situation, and the major actors were involved in a tangled web of personal and policy rivalry. One perceptive and informed Washington political reporter noted, "The fall of the shah involved a bitter though collegial contest among the President's key advisers, contending for control over foreign policy." The struggle was clearly more bitter than collegial. The primary fault line was the institutional conflict between the U.S. Department of State, directed by Secretary of State Vance, and the National Security Council, headed by adviser for national security affairs Brzezinski. In descending order of influence, the following organizations (with their respective heads listed in parentheses) were also deeply involved in the formation of Iran policy: Department of Defense (Harold Brown), Department of Energy (James Schlesinger), Central Intelligence Agency (Stansfield Turner), and Department of the Treasury (W. Michael Blumenthal). Other input was provided briefly by special adviser George Ball and, in a private and unsolicited manner, by the Rockefeller group, which included Nelson and David Rockefeller, John J. McCloy, and Henry Kissinger. The major decision-maker, and the one on whom ultimate responsibility must rest, was President Carter himself, who also sporadically sought the advice of such close associates as Vice President Walter Mondale and White House chief of staff Hamilton Jordan.

To complicate the picture further, many of the above groups were deeply divided within themselves in the recommendation of policy. This was true of both the State Department and the CIA. Also, individuals often changed their positions throughout the crisis. In order to understand the ultimate policy outcomes, it is essential to provide profiles of the most important Washington decisionmaking centers. The most complex of these was the Department of State.

The Department of State: Expertise, Division, Impotence

The chief State Department official, Vance, was a thoroughly professional and faultlessly loyal official. Cautious and judicious in approach, he mistakenly assumed that other high-level officials shared similar orientations. He was deeply preoccupied with the Camp David negotiations with Egypt and Israel and the strategic arms limitation talks with the Soviet Union, and had little time to devote to events in Iran.

In Tehran, America was represented by a tough career Foreign Service officer, William Sullivan, a distinguished, white-haired, ramrod-straight man who spoke quietly and directly. He exuded personal strength and confidence. Sullivan had just served for four years as ambassador to the Philippines, and before that he had held posts in Washington and in Southeast Asia, where it was widely rumored that he directed a wide range of American intelligence operations. He had no experience in the Middle East. Sullivan attempted to improve American intelligence in Iran but never really succeeded. By the time he made a serious effort to do so, the most extreme members of the Iranian opposition refused to have anything to do with American officials.

On November 9, 1978, Sullivan wrote his now famous cable entitled "Thinking the Unthinkable," in which he cautiously but seriously indicated that the United States had best begin preparing contingency plans in case the shah did not survive politically. Although he had come very late to the realization that the shah was unlikely to make it, he became increasingly sure of it throughout November and December 1978. He attempted to get the message to Washington, even recommending that the United States establish direct contact with Khomeini in Paris. But Sullivan found his increasingly desperate messages ignored in Washington. Not only had Brzezinski and his staff taken charge of Iran policy, but Secretary of State Vance himself refused to believe that the shah was in serious trouble. As former Under Secretary of State David Newsom has noted, "Vance was among the very last to admit, even to himself, that the shah might collapse." The fact that Sullivan received no response to his important cable of November 9 was symptomatic of the misunderstanding and lack of communication that henceforth marked Carter foreign policy toward Iran.

Brzezinski had consistently argued that only a hard-line, no-nonsense policy from the shah could save the day. Although he had been particularly slow to recognize the shah's difficulties, he always felt that tough action by the shah's military forces would scatter the opposition, which he believed consisted of Communists on the left and a few reactionary religious leaders on the right. In the bureaucratic infighting that swirled about U.S. policy toward Iran during the Carter Administration, Brzezinski, a shrewd and slashing competitor, consistently bested Secretary of State Vance, who, although principled and loyal, presented an inviting target for Brzezinski's thrusts.

By the time Vance belatedly understood what was going on in Iran, he found that Brzezinski had preempted him and had the ear of the President. Sullivan was another matter. He was at least as tough as Brzezinski. Furthermore, Sullivan was on the ground in Iran and had received some difficult on-the-job education in Iranian politics. When Brzezinski failed to respond to Sullivan's suggestions or merely took contradictory actions to those Sullivan recommended, the ambassador responded with increasingly caustic cables. Brzezinski used these to turn Carter against Sullivan. Only Vance's intervention kept Carter from firing Sullivan on the spot. This type of confrontation occurred up and down the U.S. policymaking hierarchy.

Brzezinski was generally supported by Brown and the Department of Defense, Schlesinger and the Department of Energy, and, to a somewhat lesser extent, Turner and the Central Intelligence Agency. Furthermore, several powerful American businessmen and Pahlavi supporters, such as John J. McCloy, Nelson Rockefeller and Henry Kissinger, were applying pressure on American policymakers to support the shah with whatever it took and at all costs.

A seldom-mentioned irony is that the shah himself indicated that further military measures would be counterproductive and would result in such bloodshed that his dynasty would be hated and his family's very existence would be in mortal danger. He would have nothing to do with such measures. The shah was also incredulous when he heard that Brzezinski had vetoed Sullivan's proposal that the United States make direct contact with Khomeini in Paris. After watching his troops kill over 10,000 of his own people in the streets of Iran's cities, the shah himself determined that violent tactics were doomed to fail.

Divided against itself, preoccupied with other international issues, and somewhat restrained in its capacity to do bureaucratic battle by a code of professional ethics, the Department of State watched Brzezinski and his staff arrogantly shape a policy that placed America on the losing side in a revolution. This policy seriously compromised American national interests and was partially responsible for the extremism and anti-Americanism that broke out in Iran after the revolution.

The Ball Commission

At the urging of Blumenthal and with the consent of Brzezinski, President Carter called on George Ball to carry out an independent study of the situation and to develop policy recommendations. Ball energetically began his research on November 30, 1978, and sought the advice of a wide network of Iran specialists. On at least one occasion, State Department official George Griffin managed to slip an Iran scholar up the back stairs of the White House and into Ball's office. The NSC staff did not welcome input recommended by the Department of State.

Ball prepared an 18-page memorandum for the President

entitled "Issues and Implications of the Iranian Crisis." In this hard-hitting report, Ball sharply criticized the basis of the Nixon Doctrine and stated that the United States bore much of the responsibility for the shah's megalomania. He argued that the shah was finished as an absolute monarch. Ball pointed out that military repression was doomed to fail and that it risked turning Iran into another Lebanon. Ball recommended that the shah transfer full power to a government responsive to the people. The mechanism that Ball favored for such a transfer was a Council of Notables composed of responsible individuals carefully selected by the United States. In Ball's view, "I thought this was the only way we could protect it from becoming a government of the shah's own designation." At the same time, Ball urged the President to open a disavowable channel of communication to Khomeini.

Although Ball's proposal was mild, given the lateness of the date, only Acting Secretary of State Warren Christopher gave it unqualified support. According to Ball himself, about the only positive result of his activities was that he convinced the President not to send Brzezinski to Tehran. Apparently, Brzezinski felt that his presence in Iran would provide Washington with new insights into the Iranian political scene while bolstering the courage and position of the shah. Ball incredulously told Carter that this plan, "with all due respect, is the worst idea I have ever heard."

The Huyser Mission to Iran

The Department of Defense recommended and Brzezinski supported sending a high-ranking U.S. military official to Iran as a liaison to the Iranian military forces, who seemed to hold the key to Iran's political future. The man selected was Gen. Robert "Dutch" Huyser, deputy commander in chief of the U.S. European Command under Alexander Haig. General Huyser had been traveling to Iran since the late 1960s and had close personal and professional relationships with Iranian military leaders.

Huyser's presence in Iran undercut Ambassador Sullivan's authority; it seemed evident to all that the White House now had its own representative in Tehran. Huyser's mission was a dramatic indication of Washington's two-track, collision-course, contradictory policy toward Iran. Huyser was a direct, competent officer, but he was badly over his head in the Iranian political thicket. Traveling around north Tehran in a bulletproof vest and closeted daily with five or six of the shah's leading generals, Huyser never understood Iran. He has admitted that he had never heard Khomeini's name before April 1978 and that he estimated that only 10 to 20 percent of the Iranian population supported Khomeini. Like the myopic military officers he advised, he appeared to believe that the Communists were somehow standing behind the religious leaders. While he pointed out that the Iranian generals "saw a Communist behind every mosque," he also argued "that if Iran became an Islamic Republic, it would eventually end up in the Communist camp."

High-ranking American military advisers who remained in Iran after Huyser left were shocked by the February 1979 collapse of the Iranian military. In general terms, no one should have been surprised. The military had been under incredible pressure for months. The rank-and-file soldiers were very religious and naturally susceptible to the ideas and proclamations of their clerical leaders. But even the officer class had been successfully penetrated, and a number of officers began to work quietly with the opposition. Throughout 1978 and early 1979, thousands upon thousands of soldiers had defected. By early December 1978, defections were numbering 1,000 a day.

Besides further dividing the policymaking establishment in Washington, the Huyser mission had profoundly negative effects in the Iranian political context. The opposition forces viewed Huyser's presence as an obvious U.S. attempt to intervene directly and militarily in a last-ditch effort to save the Pahlavi regime. The fact that the United States had chosen to send a senior military emissary rather than an important civilian diplomat hurt the secular moderate opposition and contributed to the extremist climate. The shah himself saw this as a hostile act designed to hasten his exit. And a small group of high-level Pahlavi loyalists in the military viewed Huyser's mission as an attempt to prevent them from staging a bloody coup in order to install a military government.

President Carter must ultimately be held responsible for the confused and confusing policy that contributed to the disastrous American foreign policy loss in Iran. An honest man of considerable intelligence, he was nonetheless at a distinct disadvantage in the intricate, constantly shifting world of foreign policy. Although he spent many, many hours studying the Iranian situation, he never understood.

Carter's Phone Call

In the eyes of the Iranian masses opposed to the shah, one of Carter's more serious political miscalculations was the timing of his telephone call to the shah after Black Friday. The shah's troops had fired into unarmed crowds at Jalah Square, killing and wounding hundreds of men, women and children on September 8, and President Carter took time out from his important Camp David meetings to call the shah early Sunday morning, September 10. Carter told the monarch that he had his personal support and friendship. This publicly announced telephone message convinced the Iranian people that Carter approved of the Jalah massacre and that the United States was now determined to oppose the revolution at all costs.

Carter's task was extremely difficult. Many of his best intelligence sources provided him with a deeply flawed and inaccurate picture of Iran. But Carter did little to improve on this record and repeated the flawed conclusions long after he should have revised his assessments. In August 1977, the CIA concluded a 60-page study with the statement that "the shah will be an active participant in Iranian life well into the 1980s" and that "there will be no radical change in Iranian political behavior in the near future." As late as September 28, 1978, the Defense Intelligence Agency reported that the shah "is expected to remain actively in power over the next 10 years." Carter himself kept repeating these rosy assessments. On December 12, 1978, the President stated: "I fully expect the shah to maintain power in Iran, and for the present problems in Iran to be resolved. . . . I think the predictions of doom and disaster that come from some sources have certainly not been realized at all. The shah has our support and he also has our confidence." On January 16, 1979, the shah fled Iran, never to return.

In his frustration and anger, Carter at times lost his cool and berated a number of his own officials. He constantly received conflicting advice and therefore wavered back and forth in his policy decisions. Although the wavering continued throughout the revolution, his general policy followed Brzezinski's advice most closely. "Carter still hoped to preserve the shah's power long after intelligence reports and top foreign policy advisers insisted, as a matter of realism, the United States must assist the orderly transition to whatever political forces were going to displace the peacock throne."

This sad state of affairs was to continue after the shah had left Iran and the United States found itself faced with the necessity of dealing with a robust, xenophobic new government in revolutionary Iran. The Carter foreign policy-making cast remained the same; only the errors differed. They were to be larger and more grievous, traumatizing the United States and searing the consciousness of the American people for 444 days.

3

Rise and Fall of the Moderates

The revolution blew the lid off the Iranian social cauldron, in which a poisonous and explosive brew of personal, political, economic and religious forces had long been fermenting. This boiling broth included the following ingredients: ethnic and tribal tensions, political repression and police brutality, institutionalized injustice and corruption, economic inefficiencies and inequities, gathering religious extremism, bureaucratic confusion and ineptitude, personal rivalry and persistent cynicism, and deepening class conflict. The forces of modernization, fueled by increasing oil revenues, outdistanced both social improvements and especially political development. As these gaps widened, the pent-up forces increased in explosive potential and burst following the final overthrow of February 1979.

When the shah left Iran on January 16, 1979, and again in mid-February when the revolution became a reality, millions of Iranians took to the streets in an ecstasy of personal and political celebration that demonstrated the depths of their disaffection. The poison that emanated from this disaffection spewed forth in many forms for years afterward. The country approached anarchy as hundreds of thousands took weapons in hand and various well-armed political groups sought to reap the rewards of their struggle against the hated Pahlavi government. Students took over the universities, workers the factories, and revolutionary committees the politics. Thousands more took this opportunity to settle personal grudges, and extremism and violence threatened to tear the country to pieces.

Peasants rose up against their landlords, sometimes killing them on the spot; mobs demolished symbols of the old system—luxury hotels, banks, cinemas and liquor stores; soldiers shot their commanding officers and took charge; the shaky new authorities began to arrest, jail and execute in the name of revolutionary "justice." When the regime attempted to slow these executions and to implement more legitimate trials, the masses demanded retribution. In Isfahan, for example, a large mob took over the central prison and massacred several high-ranking members of the former regime who were being held there. In mid-May 1979, a large delegation (including members of revolutionary tribunals and militias) visited Khomeini and demanded that either the executions continue or they would take matters into their own hands and execute all those held in the various prisons.

Arrests began February 14, and executions were implemented the next day. The primary targets of this revolutionary justice were those who most represented the instruments of repression of the Pahlavi government. These included leaders in the military, the police, SAVAK, and the prison system, along with political thugs and torturers.

This revolutionary violence was accompanied throughout by counterrevolutionary terrorism as former members of the Pahlavi system themselves became guerrillas and attacked leaders of the new regime whenever and wherever possible. The real internal war, however, did not begin until 1981, when the revolutionaries themselves confronted one another for control of the revolution. Meanwhile, the central struggle was political in nature and involved the moderate liberals and the extremist clerics. The Iranian revolution, not unlike the French and Russian revolutions, witnessed a brief postrevolutionary period in which the moderates were in the ascendancy.

The Rule of the Moderates

The last prime minister under Pahlavi rule was Shapour Bakhtiar, whose ill-fated tenure was as short as it was ineffective. An old nationalist from Musaddiq days, Bakhtiar was much more popular among American decisionmakers in Washington than he was in Iran. He held the prime ministership for less than five weeks before he fled to France. Bakhtiar's experience set the losing tone for the liberal, moderate, Westernized professionals who had entered the postrevolutionary period with high hopes.

On February 5, 1979, Ayatollah Khomeini ushered in the first stage of the Iranian revolution when he named a 73-year-old engineer to the prime ministership. The stage would end 28 months later, in June 1981. Unlike Bakhtiar, Mehdi Bazargan had impeccable opposition credentials and had spent several years in the shah's prisons. Born in 1906 to a religious family, Bazargan received his degree in thermodynamics in Paris and spent much of his intellectual energy reconciling Islamic doctrine and modern science.

Whereas Bakhtiar was willing to take office in a country in which the shah was still the titular head, Bazargan had consistently refused any such form of collaboration. He hoped to build a new government of liberal democratic form, but within a sturdy Islamic framework. This dream failed, and the old prime minister found himself constantly on the defensive as extremist opponents from both left and right sniped at his government. Bazargan and his associates were also quite willing to maintain normal diplomatic relations with the United States as long as it honored Iran's independence and autonomy. Bazargan and his closest associates even maintained close and direct contact with American governmental officials. With Bazargan's demise, moderates continued to rule under different leadership. Bazargan was replaced by a man who carried Islamic credentials while stressing the need to establish complete independence from the world's imperialism and to create a new Islamic economic system.

An intelligent, reform-minded intellectual, Abol Hassan Bani Sadr saw the answer to Pahlavi tyranny in some form of liberal Islamic state that would throw off the shackles of Western domination. Although he had met Khomeini in Najaf in the early 1970s, he did not begin a close association with the imam until Khomeini arrived as an exile in Paris in October 1978. At that time, Bani Sadr and Khomeini developed a close personal and professional relationship that would endure for 32 dramatic months.

Bani Sadr was an idealist, a bookworm and the most personally ambitious of all the liberal revolutionaries; his ego was even larger than that of Bakhtiar. Like the others, he was a representative of the professional middle class and had little rapport with or understanding of the Iranian masses. Nor did he have the skill or patience to build political organizations.

Bani Sadr returned with Khomeini to Iran, and with the imam's support he became a member of the Revolutionary Council, the Council of Experts, minister of foreign affairs, and minister of finance before he was elected Iran's first president in January 1980. Having received over 70 percent of the vote in the presidential election, Bani Sadr assumed he had a mandate from the people, failing to understand that his popularity derived mainly from Khomeini's personal support. In the last months of his presidency, he ineffectually and somewhat pathetically attempted to appeal to the Iranian people, who had little in common with a Paris-trained intellectual.

Bani Sadr's presidency was dominated by the hostage crisis, by the Iraqi invasion of September 22, 1980, and by his losing struggle against the religious extremists of the Islamic Republic party (IRP). In the end, Khomeini sided with the IRP and the clerics against Bani Sadr.

On June 21, the IRP-dominated Majlis voted to declare the president politically incompetent. The prosecutor general then ordered Bani Sadr's arrest, and he was dismissed as president on June 22. Forced into hiding, Iran's first popularly elected president fled Iran with Mujahidin-i Khalq leader Massoud Rajavi on July 29, 1981. His presidency had lasted 17 months. Thus the period of moderation ended in revolutionary Iran.

Besides their personal idiosyncracies, internal quarrels and political inexperience, the moderates were doomed to failure in

Iran for systemic reasons. They were struggling to survive in a climate in which the political winds blew strongly against them, and continually breaking events fanned extremist sentiments. These events included frontal attacks on the leaders of the revolution, threats to the territory of Iran itself, hostile actions by external forces in the regional and international contexts within which Iran acted, and natural deaths of crucial political personalities. The end of the period of the moderates was marked by full-scale violence and internal war, war that began only one week after the fall of President Bani Sadr.

The Political Strategy of Ayatollah Khomeini

When he first returned to Iran, Khomeini spent only two weeks in Tehran before moving to Qum on March 1, 1979. There is reason to believe that Khomeini fully intended to remain in Qum, where he could monitor and selectively guide the political system. This was not to be, and after nine months the imam returned to Tehran for reasons of health care and politics. Khomeini's move to Tehran center stage, however, was motivated by reasons other than simple political ambition and personal health. Close associates such as Prime Minister Bazargan persistently called on him to return to Tehran because the political situation was increasingly tenuous. In June 1979, for example, Bazargan wrote a letter to Khomeini outlining the major problems facing the revolutionary government and asking him to come to Tehran, where he could follow events more closely. Bazargan's close associates, Ibrahim Yazdi and Abbas Amir Entezam, also pressed Khomeini to return to Tehran. Politically, he was needed.

In the weeks immediately after the February 1979 overthrow, Iran threatened to collapse into anarchy. Arms were everywhere, and hundreds of factions and groupings with differing goals aspired to power. Most threatening in Khomeini's eyes were the far right and the extreme left. The counterrevolutionary right consisted of many members of the former shah's security, police and military establishments, individuals who had just lost a revolution and who now fought for their survival. Khomeini believed that such groups had readily available foreign support. The left consisted of groups even more extreme than the Mujahidin, such as the Fidayan-i Khalq and the Paykar groups. These political forces had come out of the revolution with great credibility due to their critical role in defeating the shah's Royal Guards in mid-February. Furthermore, they had a 15-year history of revolutionary resistance and an organization that was armed and intact.

Eliminating the Extreme Right and Left

Khomeini and his advisers adopted a strategy to slice off these two extremes of the political spectrum. The Fidayan, itself weakened by an internal feud that divided the movement into three parts in 1980, was an easy target since its ideology was largely anti-Islamic in nature. The counterrevolutionary right was also deeply vulnerable because of its past association with the Pahlavi regime. In 1979 and 1980, these two extremes were largely destroyed. The Mujahidin, however, was a different story. It, too, claimed commitment to Islam and had declared its loyalty to Khomeini. It was also the largest, the most dedicated, and best organized of all the groups vying for power in postrevolutionary Iran.

On June 28, 1981, a 60-pound bomb exploded in the headquarters of the IRP, killing over 100 people, including dozens of members of the Iranian political elite. The dead included the powerful founder of the IRP, Muhammad Hussein Beheshti, four cabinet ministers, six deputy ministers, and twenty-seven Majlis deputies. This shocking event initiated a full-scale internal war as the regime fought back with thousands of arrests and executions. In the ensuing cycle of violence, the opposition groups accelerated their own campaign of guerrilla terror. Their targets were the leaders of the IRP and other influential clerics, including a number of those close to Khomeini himself. On August 30, 1981, the violent opposition carried out an unprecedented assassination in which both the head of government (Prime Minister Muhammad Javad Bahonar) and the head of state (President Muhammad Ali Raja'i) died in a bombing of the Prime Ministry.

In response, the Revolutionary Guards went on a rampage and, using every means at their disposal, destroyed the armed opposition to the regime. Khomeini gave his full support to this campaign.

The June 28, 1981, attack on IRP headquarters provided Khomeini and the extremist leaders with the excuse they needed to declare war on the Mujahidin. When the Mujahidin fought back they only gave the Islamic Republic more martyrs and increased the extremism of a regime that was reminded by the death of every mullah that it was fighting for its own survival. By mid-1982, the Mujahidin were finally broken within Iran; their leader, Massoud Rajavi, had fled to Paris (and later to Iraq), and their second in command, Musa Khiabani, had been killed in a shootout in Tehran. In the process of mopping up the Mujahidin, the new ruling clerical elite also effectively and relatively easily destroyed the liberal intelligentsia, who suffocated in an atmosphere of extremism and who maintained a visceral aversion to violence.

Destruction of the Tudeh Party

Finally, in 1983 Khomeini and the IRP moved against the Tudeh party. Since the revolution, the Tudeh party had pursued a policy of political pragmatism by allying itself with Khomeini and the clerics. Traditionally aligned with the Soviet Union, this national Iranian Communist party had long suffered from its Soviet association. Still, it had a 40-year history in Iran despite the purges carried out against it by the shah's regime. During the first three years of the revolution, it supported Khomeini and the IRP while placing its members in important positions in the bureaucracy. Its members therefore exposed themselves and were well-known to the revolutionary regime. When Vladimir Kuzichkin, a Soviet diplomat and KGB major stationed in Tehran, defected to Britain in mid-1982, he provided the British with a list of several hundred Soviet agents operating in Iran. In September the official voice of the Islamic Republic, *Jumhuri-yi Islami,* sharply attacked the Tudeh party and accused it of "throwing a mouse in the soup of the revolution." Kuzichkin's information was shared with the Iranian authorities, who arrested over 1,000 Tudeh party members, many of whom had already been under surveillance. Those arrested included Nureddin Kianouri, the influential secretary-general of the Tudeh party, who publicly admitted that the party had been guilty of treason and espionage in the service of the Soviet Union. On April 30, 1983, Kianouri confessed on Iranian television that he had maintained contact with Soviet agents since 1945 and that Iranian members of the Tudeh party had been delivering top-secret military and political documents to the Soviet embassy in Tehran. On May 4, 1983, the Iranian foreign ministry announced the expulsion of 18 Soviet diplomats for interfering in the internal affairs of the Islamic Republic. This dramatic destruction of the Tudeh party in 1983 completed the dismantling of the Iranian left.

Khomeini's Legions: The Revolutionary Guards

Khomeini and his associates now needed a loyal, effective, and powerful military instrument. After purging the Pahlavi-created military officer corps, the revolutionaries established their own parallel force, the Pasdaran-i Inqilab, or Revolutionary Guards, which Khomeini had decreed into existence on May 5, 1979. This organization fought the guerrilla groups in the streets and alleys of the country. By the spring of 1982, the cleric-rulers had successfully blended the Pasdaran and the regular army into a relatively unified fighting force. After years of fighting both internal opponents and an external invader, the military forces of the Islamic Republic of Iran had become battle-hardened and experienced. Khomeini had managed to create a loyal, determined and experienced fighting force, one that had been baptized in blood and owed its very existence to him.

By 1984 the leaders of the Islamic Republic of Iran had solidified their rule with Khomeini at the center of the system. From there, the shrewd ayatollah had presided over the political consolidation of the new regime. His tactics and long-term strategy proved extremely effective. Besides being politically astute, charismatic, impeccably honest and deeply religious, Khomeini's greatest advantage was his exercise of leadership according to the traditional Shi'i mode. In this tradition, the leader seeks to understand the will of the followers and then to develop his policies accordingly. The followers in turn look to the leader for guidance and pattern their actions accordingly. In Shi'ism, therefore, it is always difficult to determine the point at which the leader leads and the follower follows. Leadership is circular rather than hierarchical. The relationships are formed within a kind of sealed circle where the leader both leads and follows and the followers both follow and lead.

In this system, Khomeini constantly sent out feelers and issued pronouncements while attempting to determine the will of the people. This often resulted both in filtering out personal considerations and in a harsh, impersonal system of repressive justice during the early years of the Islamic Republic. At times, Khomeini himself sought to introduce some moderation. A case in point was his eight-point pronouncement issued in December 1982 in which he sought to curb the excesses of overzealous, ruthless members of the system of revolutionary justice. Also, he consistently sided with the clerics of the extremist right when, representing the wishes of the deprived masses, they challenged the more secular, moderate left. Thus he ultimately jettisoned Bani Sadr, acquiesced in the execution of Sadeq Ghotbzadeh, sided with the radical students after they occupied the American embassy, and relentlessly supported the continuation of the war against Saddam Hussein's Iraq.

This form of circular leadership whereby the imam wraps himself into the masses of deprived citizens was reinforced by Khomeini's constant references to the *mustaz'afin* (deprived, dispossessed), to whom he spoke in *their* idiom while addressing *their* needs. The fact that these were the most fervently religious classes provided a powerful reinforcement for this system, a system directed by a *faqih,* or the most knowledgeable jurisprudent. From a political point of view, this system of leadership was extremely effective; it provided the imam and the new political elite with a large, dedicated constituency. This mass base of support was the primary reason for the survival of the Islamic Republic during the difficult early years of the revolution.

Khomeini never forgot that the mustaz'afin constituted the foundation of the revolution, that from these lower classes the bulk of the rank-and-file soldiers were recruited for and died in the war with Iraq. In the words of Khomeini: "To which class of society do these heroic fighters of the battlefields belong? Do you find even one person among all of them who is related to persons who have large capital, or some power in the past? If you find one, we will give you a prize. But you won't." In brief, Khomeini's priorities were always with the mustaz'afin. He clearly stated in September 1982, "We must all make efforts to serve the mustaz'afin who have been deprived throughout history and the government should always give priority to them."

'Neither East Nor West'

A final Khomeini strategy of political control was negative in nature. Like other major world revolutions, the Iranian revolution found itself immediately under attack from external forces. In Iran's case, these attacks were especially severe because both superpowers, in varying degree, supported Iraq in its war with Iran. Besides this, Iran was opposed by France, Saudi Arabia, Jordan, Egypt, Morocco, the smaller Persian Gulf states and other countries in the region. This unrelenting outside pressure acted as a coalescing force within Iran to rally the citizens around their leaders. In this sense, the external forces that sought to destroy the Iranian revolution in fact contributed to its strength and longevity. Khomeini immediately recognized the political value of these external pressures. In this context, it is important to note that the major slogan of the Iranian revolution has been Neither East nor West. In many speeches, the ayatollah stressed the external threat to Iran: "Today it seems we are left alone as almost all of the West and the East are either directly opposing us or indirectly working against us." He went on to say that Iran would fight these forces "with our bare hands and the weapons of faith."

Khomeini never relented in his condemnations and exhortations against the United States, which into the late 1980s he continued to term the Great Satan. By focusing attention on the superpower threat, he diverted attention from many of Iran's domestic problems and toward the threats emanating from "East and West." At the same time, he damaged the reputations of those individuals and groups within Iran who had associations of any kind with the superpowers and thus more easily destroyed their political power. This, in turn, only strengthened his standing among the mustaz'afin, a class with neither the will nor the capacity to develop ties of any kind with outside powers. The United States unwittingly played a critical role in this part of Khomeini's strategy. It did so by its clumsy, misguided, and counterproductive interventionist approach to Iran after the overthrow of the shah.

The traumatic revolution in Iran left U.S. decisionmakers shaken and confused. In the Department of State and in the intelligence community, American policymakers began immediately to attempt to develop a new policy toward revolutionary Iran. Several formidable obstacles confronted them. First, the United States was surprisingly ill-informed about Iran; the government did not know the players, nor did it have even a primitive understanding of the dynamics of the revolution.

Second, the Iranian scene was itself impossibly confused and deeply confusing. The political situation was in a state of explosive flux; hundreds of factions were competing for control; and emotionalism and violence were present everywhere. With the possible partial exception of Khomeini, no one, including every major Iranian actor, had any idea of where the revolution was going.

Third, a strong undercurrent of anti-Americanism ran through revolutionary Iran. This undercurrent had been fed by America's close relationship with the shah, whom the revolutionary masses considered a despotic client of the United States. Although the anti-American feeling differed in intensity from group to group in Iran, it was omnipresent and palpable from the very beginning. American decisionmakers thus had to work against a distrust in Iran that had been building for 25 years.

Finally, newly developing policy toward Iran had to be fashioned in a Washington world inhabited by powerful Pahlavi supporters. These were angry groups who blamed the Carter Administration for the fall of the shah and who were now preoccupied with thoughts of counterrevolution. Such groups sought to discredit the revolution in every way possible, portraying Iranians as uncivilized, the revolutionary leaders as barbaric and fanatical, and the revolution itself as a brief aberration that lacked popular support. A major strategy employed to condemn the revolution was to portray it as Communist-inspired and supported, with Khomeini even occasionally referred to as a "red mullah."

A Litany of Errors

The United States committed a series of major political errors during the first nine months of the revolutionary government's existence. These errors were mutually reinforcing and ultimately ended in the catastrophic hostage crisis, which brought Iranian-American relations to an all-time low and left a legacy of ill-will and animosity between the two countries. The most serious policy miscalculation was the U.S. preoccupation with the moderates. Having bet on a losing shah, the United States now placed bets on a series of moderate leaders who quickly moved to positions of power after the shah's overthrow.

The American preoccupation with the moderates was natural. These were the individuals whose liberal views most closely coincided with American political philosophy. Culturally and politically, they were sympathetic; most of their leaders spoke English, and many had been educated, if not in the United States, then in Europe. All carried impressive opposition credentials and were widely known to have struggled against the Pahlavi regime. Furthermore, the United States had established direct contact with these individuals, and embassy officials in Tehran had held many meetings with them during the late months of 1978.

The United States embraced the moderates partly by default. The Shi'i religious establishment resisted meeting with American officials. The United States had maintained no contacts with the religious leaders throughout the 1970s and, during this period, had pursued a policy clearly antithetical to the interests of the ulama. Given this background and the dominant national mood of suspicion toward the United States, it is not surprising that the religious leaders were reluctant to respond enthusiastically to American overtures.

The American belief in the moderates led the government to sponsor a policy of cautious support and increased contacts with the shaky new political elite then emerging in immediate post-Pahlavi Iran. The Department of State and other U.S. agencies gradually built a new, if smaller, presence in Iran, beginning in midsummer of 1979. In an attempt to improve on past performance, the latest group of official Americans posted to Iran were determined to get in touch with as many Iranians as possible.

Many Iranian revolutionaries watched this mutual embrace sullenly and with growing concern. They believed that the violent revolution against the shah had also been carried out to destroy American influence in the political affairs of their country. Suddenly, Americans were back and active. That U.S. officials were apparently allying themselves with Western-educated liberals concerned them even more. The groups most concerned about the U.S. presence were the radical left and the extremist religious right, with whom the United States had little rapport. In its enthusiasm and desire to rescue itself from a bad situation, the United States failed to reenter Iran cautiously and discreetly.

Moderates' Disaffection

Despite its new, active political presence in Iran, the United States failed to establish any meaningful relationships with the major extremist religious leaders. At the White House there was a stubborn resentment of Khomeini, a petulant attitude that resulted in a consistent refusal to approach the central leader of the revolution. Although it is of course questionable whether Khomeini would have been willing to meet the U.S. officials, experienced American Foreign Service officers later argued strongly that the failure to contact Khomeini was a diplomatic error of major proportions.

The policy toward Khomeini is symptomatic of the overall attitude of the United States toward the Iranian revolution. A certain bitterness and hostility were evident from the beginning. The acceptance of the revolution was grudging at best, and this was quite clear to the revolutionaries. The evidence went far deeper than the failure to open communications with Khomeini. It began with the refusal of the United States even to acknowledge publicly the revolution.

Besides alienating the extremists, the United States ironically also succeeded in deeply disturbing the moderates, the very group that American decisionmakers hoped to court and to strengthen politically. If the United States professed to support them, the moderates themselves argued this was indeed a strange sort of support. In their view there had been no strong statements in support of the revolution, no willingness to admit possible past foreign policy errors, no resupply of badly needed spare parts (spare parts already paid for), no willingness to consider extradition of political criminals or the repatriation of Pahlavi funds and no serious attempt to cooperate with the real leadership of the Iranian revolution. In exasperation, almost desperation, the moderates constantly complained to American diplomats about these unfriendly acts of political omission.

The situation was further exacerbated by U.S. intelligence activities conducted in Iran after the revolution. Two episodes loomed especially large in shaping the subsequent state of U.S.-Iranian relations. The first was a CIA plan to develop a liaison with Bani Sadr; the second was a more general CIA plan designed to establish close working relationships with the moderate faction within the Iranian revolutionary establishment. Both plans were rather crudely designed and heavy-handed, and both contributed to the dramatic failure of the moderates and to the final collapse of American credibility in Iran. They became known to the Iranian extremists in late 1979–early 1980 after the student groups gained access to secret documents upon occupying the U.S. embassy in Tehran. These documents then became a powerful political tool used by the revolutionary extremists to bludgeon the moderates, who were now demonstrated to have had close associations with American intelligence officials.

4

The Hostage Crisis

On the night of October 22, 1979, a Gulfstream aircraft landed quietly at La Guardia airport in New York City. The jet carried the shah and empress of Iran and a small royal entourage. Hours earlier, President Carter had given the approval for the shah to enter the United States for medical treatment. This momentous decision led directly to a new era in Iranian-American relations—an era dominated by extremism, distrust, hatred and violence. Carter had resisted admitting the shah to the United States for nine pressure-packed months, but he finally relented in the face of formidable pressures, including persistent lobbying for admission by the shah's powerful friends in America, genuine humanitarian considerations and political calculations involving the forthcoming 1980 presidential election. Carter later described the circumstances surrounding his decision: "I was told that the shah was desperately ill, at the point of death. I was told that New York City had the only medical facility that was capable of possibly saving his life and reminded that the Iranian officials had promised to protect our people in Iran. When all the circumstances were described to me, I agreed."

Despite dire predictions by Iran specialists about a swift anti-American response in Iran, the reaction at first was curiously muted after the admission became known to Iranians. It seemed to take some days for the significance of this event to sink into the revolutionary consciousness. Meanwhile, other American political actions only heightened the distrust and increased the tension; for example, the meeting in Algiers between national security adviser Brzezinski and Bazargan, Ibrahim Yazdi and Mustafa Chamran on November 1. The Algiers meeting, especially, deepened the anti-American paranoia and shortened the political life of the moderates.

Given the paranoia rampant in Iran and the shah's recent admission to the United States, the Algiers meeting was a severe political miscalculation. Both Brzezinski, who was consistently insensitive to events taking place in Iran, and the Iranian officials, who should have known better, erred in participating in this session. On that day, November 1, 1979, huge revolutionary demonstrations with a heavy anti-American flavor took place in Tehran. Approximately 2 million angry demonstrators shouted "Death to America" and listened to fiery speeches denouncing the United States for harboring "the criminal shah." That evening, Iranian National Television showed pictures of Brzezinski shaking hands with the Iranian delegation. The Iranian extremists interpreted this as evidence of the Bazargan government's collusion with an America that had just given refuge to the shah, whom they held responsible for all their problems. Years after the revolution both sides still vehemently claim that the other requested the meeting.

On November 4, 1979, less than two weeks after the shah was admitted to the United States and less than three days after the Algiers meeting, a group of nearly 500 extremist students attacked the U.S. embassy in Tehran, initially taking 61 Americans hostage. For the next 444 days, American citizens watched in helpless anger and horror as Iranian extremists held 52 of the American officials hostage in Tehran. American-Iranian relations had sunk to an all-time low.

It now seems certain that the militants had plans to move on the

Muslim militants paint the entrance of the occupied U.S. embassy in Tehran to celebrate the first anniversary of the seizure of the American hostages.

UPI/Bettmann Newsphotos

American embassy in Tehran long before November 4 and that they put their plans into action when anti-American rhetoric and feeling began to peak in the first three days of that month. Although the embassy takeover may have been planned in advance, the actual operation involved different leaders from those who laid the plans and factions with unclear long-term goals. Ayatollah Khomeini himself at first quietly expressed disapproval of the move but later became a strong supporter when he realized the overwhelming popularity of the act among the Iranian masses. There is evidence that the students themselves were astonished by the responses their action elicited, both within Iran and around the world.

As the Carter Administration overreacted and the American mass media turned its complete attention on the event, the student extremists quickly recognized the influence they had suddenly attained. While the American giant shouted and threatened the lawbreakers before the eyes of the world, the extremists stubbornly refused to budge and, in traditional bazaar bargaining-style, only increased the price for any accommodation. In Iran, the moderate-extremist struggle intensified, and the former lost ground rapidly. Prime Minister Bazargan resigned on November 6, and the moderates who had communicated with the United

States were left powerless. Bani Sadr was also politically impotent. Deeply upset by the taking of diplomatic hostages, most middle-class Iranian moderates found themselves sitting on the sidelines watching American bluster deepen the international crisis and increase the credibility of the extremists in Tehran.

Embassy Takeover Triggers Political Infighting

The hostage incident occasioned three major political power struggles within Iran. The most general confrontation was the conflict between the extremists and the moderates. The incident demonstrated that the extremists had mass support while the moderates lacked credibility at the grass roots of society. The second struggle overlapped the first and involved the formal governmental apparatus represented by the IRP on the one hand and the student militants within the embassy compound on the other hand. The embassy takeover presented the IRP with a *fait accompli*. Nonetheless, tension persisted between the government and the students. The former privately warned the militants that if any of the hostages were to die, the student captors would themselves pay with their lives. The third and most specific power struggle occurred within the embassy grounds, where the students formed various factions, including those of the radical left and right.

Although the religious extremists outnumbered the students of Marxist inclination, the latter were in many ways more desperate and therefore more likely to take some dramatic retributive acts against an American prisoner. There was serious danger, especially during the beginning months, that such an act might occur, thereby forcing military confrontation between Iran and the United States. Such an act would have introduced a new level of conflict—war—and would have benefited both the radical left within Iran and quite possibly the Soviet Union, monitoring events closely from the north. Partly because of this danger, the left was gradually purged from within the student ranks, and the Islamic extremists took control.

The embassy takeover reinforced the extremist phase of the revolution because it continued to radicalize the rules of politics in

Iran. The continuing process of radicalization was fed from two directions, from within and from without. The militants were certain in their own minds that the embassy was a center of American espionage, a "nest of spies" (*laneh-yi jasusi*), as they termed it. On taking the embassy, they captured thousands of pages of diplomatic documents and correspondence. They immediately began to piece together the documents that had been shredded and initiated a thorough study of what they had discovered. Less than a month after they had occupied the U.S. embassy, the student extremists began to release the captured documents for internal political purposes, slowly and effectively, until by 1988 some 60 volumes had been published.

The evidence that they thought they had found in the U.S. embassy was enough to reinforce their perceptions that once again America was interfering in Iranian internal affairs, that it was in touch with moderate Western-educated leaders, that it had long intended to admit the shah into the United States, and that it was, therefore, fundamentally hostile to the Iranian revolution.

One series of revelations that contributed greatly to the fear of the revolutionaries was released in fall 1984 and spring 1985. Embassy documents showed that American and Soviet diplomats had been meeting and comparing notes in Tehran restaurants throughout the revolution. The content of the discussions is very revealing and indicates that both the United States and the U.S.S.R. were deeply troubled by the unrest in Iran and that neither country was very well informed about what was taking place before their very eyes.

The documents provided the Iranian religious revolutionaries with what they considered to be incontrovertible evidence that the world's two superpowers had colluded in supporting the shah and in opposing the revolution. Although they never required a smoking gun to support their theories of external interference, the Iranians now felt they had one. That the Soviet finger seemed to have helped the American finger pull the trigger did not lessen anti-Americanism in Iran in the slightest.

Iranian hostility deepened as the Carter Administration desperately engaged in numerous activities designed to force Iran to release the hostages. The application of pressure only increased the determination of the hostage holders, whose popularity grew at home in direct proportion to the amount of pressure applied by the United States. As America became mesmerized by and preoccupied with the hostage situation, President Carter found himself under enormous pressure to take decisive action.

The Abortive Rescue Mission

Throughout early 1980 the Carter Administration debated a rescue mission and strike into Iran. Secretary of State Vance and the Department of State generally opposed the plan, arguing that it would fail, that it could result in the loss of many lives, and that, in the end, it would play into the hands of the Khomeini regime. On April 11, 1980, the President held a special meeting of the NSC at which it was decided to go ahead with the raid into Iran. This important meeting took place while Vance was away on vacation in Florida. His place at the meeting was taken by Deputy Secretary Christopher, who had no knowledge of the rescue mission before he attended the session. Vance was not informed of the decision until he returned to Washington from vacation. He again voiced his misgivings and opposition to Carter. He vowed to tender his resignation once the rescue attempt had taken place.

At 7:30 P.M. on April 24, 1980, eight Sea Stallion RH-53D helicopters lifted off from the aircraft carrier *Nimitz* deployed in the Arabian Sea off the coast of southeastern Iran. The helicopters were to fly 600 miles to Desert One, a remote landing strip some 275 miles southeast of Tehran. Here they were to rendezvous with six C-130 Hercules transport planes, and the rescue team was to prepare for another trip to Desert Two, from which the commandos were to board vans and trucks for the 50-mile ride into Tehran. This ill-fated operation named Eagle Claw never proceeded beyond Desert One; it was aborted in the early hours of the following morning. In the course of the operation, three of the eight helicopters were rendered inoperable, and one of them sliced into a C-130, setting both crafts aflame and killing eight American servicemen. A hurried exit in the C-130s resulted in the abandonment of helicopters, weapons, maps and secret documents. The entire adventure was an embarrassing tragedy of errors, the details of which remain little known in the United States.

In Washington, having failed in one attempt, Brzezinski boldly and immediately began to make plans for another military adventure. But President Carter appointed Senator Edmund S. Muskie (D-Me.) to replace Vance, who had resigned as promised, and now placed all emphasis on diplomatic tactics. Muskie's low-key negotiating approach, along with changing political exigencies in Iran and the United States, ultimately resulted in the release of the hostages on January 20, 1981. The final agreement was complex and involved both political promises and reciprocal economic and international banking arrangements. Although many Americans proclaimed the release and agreement a victory, the hostage episode was, if anything, a serious defeat for American foreign policy.

The hostage crisis left a legacy of distrust, misunderstanding and hatred that will plague Iranian-American relations for years. In this sense, both sides are losers. The collapse of American power in the Iranian desert in April 1980 rankled U.S. military and political leaders, who waited for the opportunity to score a dramatic success in their relations with Iran. According to the testimony of NSC officials during the July 1987 congressional hearings on the Iran-contra affair, it was the lingering embarrassment of this adventure in 1980 that helped promote the ill-fated arms for hostages initiative of 1985–86. Such is the manner in which mistakes of the past smooth the way for policy errors in the future.

Within the short-term context of Iranian revolutionary politics, on the other hand, there is little doubt that the militants and extremists gained a great deal from the hostage episode. They used it effectively to take control of a revolution. The United States became their unwitting ally by publicizing the event far out of proportion to its significance in the world of politics, by personalizing and moralizing, by threatening and posturing, and by attacking Iran in a rescue attempt that was fatally flawed in both planning and execution.

Khomeini had long been warning the Iranian people of an impending American attack. To the Iranians, the failed rescue attempt proved this prediction to be correct and greatly enhanced Khomeini's credibility. Khomeini pointed out that even the mighty United States with all its modern technology had fallen before a God who was acting as Iran's protector.

The hostage-taking served five interrelated purposes for the Iranian revolutionary extremists. First and foremost, as emphasized above, it enabled the extremist factions to gain the ascendancy over the moderates. Second, it provided the religious extremists with the political opportunity and capital to defeat the radical challenge from the left. By taking strong and dramatic action against the United States, the militant religious forces preempted the threat of the radical left. Third, it rallied the masses of Iranian people behind the revolution by providing them with the constant specter of a powerful external opponent. Fourth, it provided the revolutionaries with hostages against the perceived threat of an imminent American act to reverse the revolution. Finally, it provided retribution. A weaker country had taken direct action against a superpower—a superpower whose outcries provided daily evidence of its embarrassment and political impotence.

Once the hostages were released, even the Department of State chose to ignore what had happened. In the words of John Limbert, an extremely talented Iran specialist and former hostage: "*No one* spoke to any of the Persian-speaking political officers among the hostages to find out what happened and who the captors were. It wasn't until April 1981 after several of us had urged such a meeting that it was organized. My overall impression is that most officials, with a few exceptions, just didn't care." A serious examination of what had happened and why would certainly have uncovered many unpalatable truths. It would have also done America an enormous favor by providing a badly needed explanation so that errors, oversights, and misunderstandings made in the past may not necessarily have to be repeated.

5

The Iran-Iraq War

On September 22, 1980, Iraqi troops invaded Iran along a 400-mile front while Iraqi aircraft carried out strikes against a dozen Iranian airfields. When the Iraqis struck, the Iranian revolution was at a low point and intense internal power struggles were in progress in Tehran. The economy was extremely fragile; the Kurds were in revolt in the northwest; and counterrevolutionary forces of all kinds were actively committing acts of terrorism. Also, the hostage crisis was ongoing, and the United States was applying severe international pressure on the Iranian government. While there is little doubt that the Iranian regime was engaging in provocative broadcasts and propaganda against Iraq, it is also true that Iraq invaded Iran and was by any standard of international law the aggressor.

The attack caught revolutionary Iran by surprise. Nonetheless, Iran responded quickly and poured reinforcements into the southwest, where badly outnumbered Iranian soldiers, police and citizens were fighting a desperate war of defense. After a month of brutal hand-to-hand fighting and very heavy casualties, the city of Khorramshahr fell to the invaders. This was the only major Iranian city to fall to the Iraqis; in May 1982 it was retaken by

Iranian forces. Having slowed the invasion and having mobilized and consolidated their forces, the Iranians counterattacked in the fall of 1981 and spring of 1982. In two major battles fought in the area of Dezful in March–April 1982 and in Khorramshahr in April–May 1982, the Iranian troops won important victories, driving the Iraqis off most Iranian soil. In this offensive, the Iranians managed to coordinate the activities of 100,000 regular troops, 30,000 Revolutionary Guards and another 30,000 members of the popular militia.

During 1983 Iran again went on the offensive, attempting to drive onto Iraqi soil and hoping for a breakthrough that would destroy the regime of Saddam Hussein in the capital city of Baghdad. These invasions were largely failures, and the war degenerated into a campaign of massive Iranian human-wave attacks on fixed Iraqi positions protected by millions of deadly mines and a modern computerized Iraqi defense, dug in and covering Iranian advances with overlapping fields of fire. In this struggle of man against machine, the casualty numbers were staggering. With the possible exception of World War I, the casualties as percentages of population figures have been the highest of any war in this century. As the longest Middle East war in recent history, the Iran-Iraq conflict has resulted in an estimated 400,000 deaths and 1 million wounded on the Iranian side and 300,000 deaths and 900,000 wounded on the Iraqi side. By 1987 Iran had suffered more battle deaths than the United States in World War II, and Iran had only one third the population that America had in 1945. Reliable sources indicate that by 1988 the economic costs of the conflict were already as high as $800 billion.

Between 1983 and 1988 Iran began to change its military strategy to stress a war of attrition. Unrelenting pressure was put on the Iraqis, who, with a much smaller population, were already stretched very thinly along a 400-mile line of defense. This new Iranian policy of probing, pushing and pressuring resulted in two highly successful limited offensives in February 1984 and February 1986. In the first, Iran managed to take Iraq's oil-rich Majnun Islands, and in the second Iran captured the southern

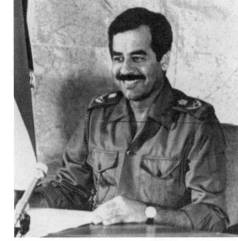

Iraqi President Saddam Hussein: Iran has made the removal from power of the man who initiated the war a precondition for peace negotiations.

UPI/Bettmann Newsphotos

port city of Fao and held it until April 1988. In January 1987 the war once again escalated sharply as Iran mounted successive attacks against the besieged southern Iraqi city of Basra. These sharp, bloody probes cost both countries dearly as Iran continued to pursue its strategy of selective military pressure.

'War of the Cities'

Ever since the successful Iranian counterattacks of 1983, the Iraqi regime has attempted to convince Iran to participate in peace talks. When Iran has refused, the government of Saddam Hussein has sought to force Iran to the conference table. A major example of this tactic occurred in February and March of 1985, when Iraq threw all its might at Iran. This "war of the cities" involved Iraqi air attacks on 40 Iranian cities (including Tehran), Scud and Frog missile strikes on population centers, chemical and gas attacks, increased strikes against Kharg Island and attacks on Persian Gulf shipping. In the spring of 1988, Iraq again intensified the war, this time launching surface-to-surface missiles outfitted with booster rockets directly into Tehran while also unleashing deadly poisonous gas attacks along the northern front.

These tactics failed badly: Iranians responded to the punishment by rallying around their leaders and increasing their determination to fight Iraq to the bitter end. Iraq's attacks on civilian centers and its use of poisonous gases have clearly failed to influence the Iranian leaders and masses. If anything, such actions have only prolonged the war.

Despite occasional reports to the contrary, the Islamic Republic of Iran has been consistent in its conditions for an end to the war: (1) that Iraq withdraw its troops from all Iranian soil; (2) that Iraq pay reparations for the damage done to Iran as a result of the invasion; and (3) that Saddam Hussein be removed from power in Iraq. As the war dragged on into 1988, it became increasingly clear that war-weary Iran would be willing to enter into negotiations with Iraq if Saddam Hussein were to disappear from the scene. Part of the reason for the Saddam-must-go demand is that the Iranian leaders feel that they cannot negotiate with the man who initiated the war and who is responsible for so much Iranian bloodshed. In the view of Ayatollah Khomeini: "If we ignore Iraq's aggression, we have ignored a spiritual matter, that is, we have encouraged an oppressor."

U.S. Policy Vacillations

From the beginning of the Persian Gulf war, American policymakers were divided over what position the United States should assume in the conflict. For the first two years of the war, America took a position of strict neutrality. With the successful Iranian military campaigns of 1982 and the subsequent offensives against Iraq, policymakers began to fear an outright Iranian victory. Beginning in mid-1983, the United States moved to support Iraq.

The United States had removed Iraq from its list of countries considered supportive of international terrorism in 1982. High-level American officials began to visit Baghdad in late 1983, and the United States subsequently extended Iraq approximately $2 billion in commodity credits. Beginning in 1984, it became widely known that Iraq was benefiting from intelligence supplied through American sources. Saddam Hussein himself flatly stated in May 1984 that Iraq had the use of intelligence provided by AWACS aircraft flown by American pilots based in Saudi Arabia. On November 26, 1984, the United States restored diplomatic relations with Iraq after a 17-year break. When Iraqi-fired Exocet sea-skimming missiles struck the American frigate U.S.S. *Stark* in the Persian Gulf on May 17, 1987, killing 37 American sailors, the Reagan Administration quickly accepted the official Iraqi statement that the attack was "inadvertent." President Reagan afterward stated curiously that "Iran is the real villain in the piece," and his Administration issued a series of sharp warnings to Iran. In a May 27, 1987, press conference, the President crudely referred to Iran as "this barbaric country."

These words and deeds understandably increased Iran's alienation from America. To Iran's leaders, the United States was continuing its hostile, counterrevolutionary policy and apparently intended to use every means at its disposal to destroy the Islamic Republic. Iran's leaders often referred to what they considered an obvious American double standard. Why had the United States never condemned Iraq's original attack in 1980 while it consistently criticized Iran's counteroffensives? Why did the United States sharply condemn revolutionary Iranian justice while it said not a word about the brutally repressive regime of Saddam Hussein? Why did America claim its intention to protect shipping in the southern Gulf from Iranian attacks while it tolerated the much more frequent Iraqi attacks in the northern Gulf? Why had the United States blamed Iran for the blatant Iraqi missile attack on the U.S.S. *Stark*?

Arms for Hostages

With the exception of Syria and the partial exceptions of Libya and Algeria, Iran found itself quite alone. This international isolation, along with the accumulating pressures of the war and the alarming Soviet occupation of Afghanistan next door, led Iranian leaders in 1985–86 to participate in a secret rapprochement with the United States, involving hostages, spare parts, secret American envoys and a sordid assortment of international middlemen that broke into a major scandal in November 1986.

Beginning in 1985, a small group of high-ranking NSC officials started implementing their own policy toward Iran. With the encouragement of President Reagan himself, and with the cooperation of the CIA, headed by William Casey, these officials sought to sell Iran badly needed arms and spare parts. In return Iran was expected to assist in the release of American hostages held in Lebanon. This program ran directly counter to State Department policy, but it received the formal approval of President Reagan in the Presidential Finding he signed on January 17, 1986.

The secret, limited rapprochement was spearheaded initially by national security adviser McFarlane with the strong backing of Casey. McFarlane's actions were encouraged by consultants such as Michael Ledeen, who maintained close Israeli connections. Along with the Israelis, Ledeen urged the NSC to work with Manuchehr Ghorbanifar, an Iranian citizen and private entrepreneur alleged to have been a former employee of SAVAK. Ghorbanifar had been considered unreliable by American intelligence in 1980–82, and he failed a CIA-administered lie detector test in January 1986, showing "deception on virtually all of the relevant questions." Yet, although deeply distrusted, he continued for some time to represent America's line to Iran. Part of the reason concerned his sponsorship by Israel and by Ledeen, who described him as a "wonderful man . . . almost too good to be true" and "one of those rare individuals who understands not only the subtleties of his own culture but our own as well." Ledeen's confidence notwithstanding, the polygraph report concluded that "Ghorbanifar is clearly a fabricator and wheeler-dealer who has undertaken activities prejudicial to U.S. interests."

After McFarlane was replaced in December 1985 as NSC head by Vice Adm. John M. Poindexter, Poindexter and powerful operative Lt. Col. North carried the plan forward. The key event in the project occurred on May 25, 1986, when McFarlane, North, NSC Middle East adviser Howard Teicher, Israeli Amiram Nir, George Cave of the CIA and others flew into Tehran to exchange arms for American hostages in Lebanon.

Tom Toles for *The Buffalo News*

With the partial exception of Cave, who was brought into the project rather late in the game, Iranian expertise was notably absent. Government Iran specialists in the middle echelons of the Department of State had been frozen out of the picture both by Shultz's adamant opposition to any rapprochement with Iran and by the understanding at the NSC that such individuals would only oppose the project. The plan was cobbled together in an atmosphere of arrogance and ignorance.

Despite profound ignorance and tactical blunders, one might argue that the attempt to develop a line of communication with Iran was in America's strategic interests. A number of complex and interrelated considerations lay behind the decision to approach Iran—seven in all. Two were tactical, three were strategic, and two were external. The tactical reasons involved the hostages and the substance of intelligence reports. The strategic reasons focused on the Soviet challenge, the fear of the forceful exportation of the Iranian revolution to other Gulf states, and the issue of petroleum prices. The two external contributing reasons involved support for the plan in both Israel and Iran itself.

One tactical reason involved the personal alarm and political impotence that Reagan and a number of his advisers felt over the American hostages held in Lebanon. According to Chief of Staff Donald Regan, the President wanted to keep the arms for hostages initiative going "not only for geopolitical reasons but also the fact that we weren't getting anywhere in getting more hostages out. And we were going to spend another Christmas with hostages there, and he is looking powerless and inept as President because he's unable to do anything to get the hostages out." Reagan's preoccupation with hostages was clearly both humanitarian and political. The return of hostage Benjamin Weir on September 15, 1985, just after two Israeli shipments of arms to Tehran, kept the initiative alive. The United States quietly condoned and approved these arms transfers.

A second tactical reason for the overture to Iran involved U.S. intelligence reports. In May 1985 Graham Fuller, the CIA's national intelligence officer for the Near East, prepared a memorandum warning that Iran was in severe danger of disintegration, that Khomeini's position was faltering, and that the U.S.S.R. was poised to take advantage of this possible collapse. NSC analysts Teicher and Donald Fortier reinforced this position in a June National Security Decision Directive (NSDD). These reports represented the fusion of ideas of the CIA and NSC and provided the intellectual rationale for the overture to Iran. The Iran initiative was continued through 1986, when further intelligence studies reportedly indicated that Iran was now gaining the upper hand in the war with Iraq. Given its past tilt to the Iraqi side in the conflict, where would the United States be if Iran should win the war? To hedge its bets, the United States pursued a contradictory, two-track policy toward Iran.

The first important strategic reason for the overture to Iran concerned the White House preoccupation with Soviet power in the Gulf region. Teicher's NSDD of June 17, 1985, stressed repeatedly the Soviet threat to Iran and to America's interests in the region. These views were reinforced by influential advisers such as Regan, who argued that the President felt "that we cannot allow Iran to fall into the Soviet camp."

The second strategic concern was the danger that Iran would export its revolution to neighboring conservative Gulf states. America was especially worried about stability in Saudi Arabia, a country with one quarter of the world's proven reserves of petroleum. By 1985 it had become increasingly clear that the Iranian revolution was a fact of life. It was time to work for commitments from the Islamic Republic that it would not attempt to destabilize these oil-rich traditional governments. According to the Reagan Administration itself, during the negotiations throughout most of 1986, there were no Iran-sponsored incidents of terrorism.

The final strategic reason was an economic one. Throughout much of 1986, oil prices had plummeted until they bottomed out at less than $10 per barrel. This occurred primarily as a result of sharply increased Saudi production that cut severely into the revenues of the major oil-producing states. In the Middle East, Iran's and America's interests converged on this issue. Within the councils of OPEC, the Islamic Republic had been struggling for lower production and higher prices. The United States, meanwhile, needed prices high enough to protect the domestic oil industry but low enough to placate the consumer. The surprise Saudi-Iranian agreement on lower production in August–September 1986 achieved this goal, and prices rose steadily to the $18 per barrel level in 1987.

Israel's Agenda

As a major external contributing cause for the U.S. initiative in 1985–86, Israel was of course pursuing its own self-interest. Israel had long been shipping arms and spare parts to Iran on its own. By drawing the United States into the project, the Israelis hoped to gain American legitimacy for their goal of penetrating the leadership of the Islamic Republic of Iran.

The final contributing reason for the American approach to Iran is Iran itself. The arrangement was grudgingly approved at the highest levels of the Iranian government and had the tacit consent of Khomeini, who was genuinely concerned about the survival of the Islamic Republic. From the Iranian side, it was part of a steady movement toward political pragmatism, which had been slowly replacing the ideological extremism dominant since the revolution. When the extremist factions in Iran saw themselves weakened by such developments, a group in their camp responded in October 1986 by leaking the story of the arms-for-hostages dealings. Only the direct intervention of Khomeini himself held the domestic political situation steady after these revelations. Iran was committed to a new relationship with the United States; after the original Ghorbanifar-Israel channel had been closed down, the Islamic Republic supported a second channel that it considered free from Israeli contamination.

Wise Strategy, Flawed Execution

The reasons for the American overture to Iran are compelling when viewed from a strategic perspective. The American eagle cannot afford to be out of communication with the Iranian lion, the most powerful force in the Persian Gulf. Yet the methodology of the plan to establish this communication was poorly, clumsily and unprofessionally conceived. It involved the wrong people (McFarlane, North, Teicher) advised by the wrong "experts" (Ledeen, Ghorbanifar) supported by the wrong ally (Israel); they went to the wrong place (Tehran) at the wrong time (during the month of Ramadan and after the United States had tilted to the Iraqi side in the Gulf war), carrying the wrong tactical plan. The unprofessional and uninformed nature of this adventure jeopardized the credibility and political survival of both American and Iranian leaders, dealt another serious blow to the fading credibility of the United States in the international arena, and, in the process, threatened to freeze Iranian-American relations for another decade.

On the other hand, Khomeini and other Iranian leaders

concluded in the mid-1980s that the Islamic Republic needed to resume relations with the United States. If such relations involved respect for one another's territorial integrity and national autonomy, if the United States retreated from its hostility toward the revolution and adopted a position of strict neutrality in the Gulf war, then Iran would accept a normalization of relations. Prodded by their immediate need for arms and spare parts, the Iranians sought lines to the United States in 1985–86.

A Common Need to Communicate

On the American side, the Islamic Republic of Iran is still largely viewed as a reactionary, repressive government directed by extremists, terrorists and fanatics. Reagan's protestations that the United States had evidence that Iran had begun to change its terrorist ways met with disbelief and anger by most American political leaders and by the public. The hostage episode, in particular, will shape America's views of revolutionary Iran for years to come. The pleas of many informed Americans, including a number of the hostages themselves, such as John Limbert, Barry Rosen and Charles Scott, that the United States make an effort to understand the Iranian position, have largely fallen on deaf ears. Although the Iranian arms affair demonstrated that American leaders had momentarily begun to rethink the country's Iran policy, the aftermath of the Iraqi missile strike against the U.S.S. *Stark* revealed the reality of continuing American hostility toward Iran. As part of this tense atmosphere that developed following the Iran-contra revelations, the Reagan Administration began reflagging Kuwaiti oil tankers and providing them with military escort service in July 1987. By mid-1988, the United States and Iran were involved in sporadic firefights in the Gulf. This projection of American military power directly into the Persian Gulf revealed a new level of support for Iraq in its conflict with Iran.

The tragedy of America and Iran is that each side—the large numbers of Iranians committed to the Islamic Republic and most patriotic Americans—has failed to understand the other's point of view. Meanwhile, the governments of both countries develop their foreign policy in an atmosphere of paranoia, hatred, ignorance and emotion. The clumsy and costly early attempts by both sides to cautiously reestablish relations have resulted in further misunderstanding and have shaken the credibility of both political systems. Nevertheless, there are signs that deep down both countries feel a common need to communicate and cooperate. Although the 1986–87 revelations have set the timetable back, there will be another attempt. Until that succeeds, both the eagle and the lion will suffer as they confront one another in a tense and tumultuous world.

Talking It Over

A Note for Students and Discussion Groups

This issue of the HEADLINE SERIES, like its predecessors, is published for every serious reader, specialized or not, who takes an interest in the subject. Many of our readers will be in classrooms, seminars or community discussion groups. Particularly with them in mind, we present below some discussion questions—suggested as a starting point only—and references for further reading.

Discussion Questions

What key event soured Iranian goodwill toward the United States?

What lessons should the United States have learned in dealing with the shah? Did it apply these lessons in future dealings with other authoritarian rulers, such as President Ferdinand Marcos of the Philippines or President Jean-Claude Duvalier of Haiti?

Discuss the difference between American and Iranian perceptions of what was happening during the Iranian revolution. How did the shah's opponents view U.S. policy?

How was U.S. policy toward Iran formulated? Discuss the different viewpoints of the major actors. How did the United States get information about what was happening in Iran?

How much influence do you think the United States had to shape the course of the Iranian revolution? Could Washington have saved the shah? Should the United States have been prepared to intervene?

The United States was caught by surprise by the strength of the Islamic revival in Iran and by its anti-American tone. How should the United States deal with religious movements in other countries, such as Afghanistan or Poland?

The hostage-taking by Iran resulted in unprecedented media coverage of a country that had previously been little known. Did such coverage help prolong the crisis? How did it affect coverage of future terrorist acts, such as the hijacking of the *Achille Lauro* in October 1985?

How important a bearing should human rights concerns have on U.S. policy? How would you assess the role of human rights in the foreign policies of Presidents Carter and Reagan?

The United States is often tempted to intervene in revolutionary situations in the Third World where it believes its interests are threatened. What guidelines should the U.S. follow in such situations? Would it be an advantage or disadvantage for the United States to support publicly moderate elements?

Iraq attacked Iran in September 1980, starting a costly war which has no end in sight. Why has U.S. policy favored Iraq? What are the prospects for a U.S. rapprochement with Iran? Should the United States care who wins the war?

The Iran-contra affair revealed that the United States pursued two policies, one official and one secret, that were contradictory. What are the perils of conducting policy in such a way?

READING LIST

Abrahamian, Ervand, *Iran Between Two Revolutions*. Princeton, N.J., Princeton University Press, 1982. A superb contemporary history of Iran that focuses on political movements and social forces.

Algar, Hamid, *Islam and Revolution: Writings and Declarations of Imam Khomeini*. Berkeley, Calif., Mizan Press, 1981. A carefully compiled and translated collection of Khomeini's major statements by an eminent interpreter of Shi'i Islam.

Amirahmadi, Hooshang, and Parvin, Manoucher, eds., *Post-Revolutionary Iran*. Boulder, Colo., Westview Press, 1988. A recent collection of articles containing much new material on the Islamic Republic of Iran.

Bakhash, Shaul, *The Reign of the Ayatollahs: Iran and the Islamic Revolution*. New York, Basic Books, 1984. A meticulously researched study of the early years of the Iranian revolution.

Bill, James A., *The Eagle and the Lion: The Tragedy of American-Iranian Relations*. Yale University Press, 92A Yale Station, New Haven, CN 06520. $25, cloth. Book from which this HEADLINE SERIES is excerpted.

————, and Louis, Wm. Roger, eds., *Musaddiq, Iranian Nationalism and Oil*. London, England, I.B. Tauris, 1988. An original collection of articles that analyze all dimensions of the important Musaddiq movement of 1951–53.

Dorman, William A., and Farhang, Mansour, *The U.S. Press and Iran: Foreign Policy and the Journalism of Deference*. Berkeley, University of California Press, 1987. A hard-hitting, reliable study that documents the failure of the American mass media to report accurately and responsibly on Pahlavi Iran.

Ioannides, Christos P., *America's Iran: Injury and Catharsis*. Lanham, Md., University Press of America, 1984. A competent concise analysis of the rupture of American-Iranian relations.

Keddie, Nikki R., *Roots of Revolution: An Interpretive History of Modern Iran* (with a section by Yann Richard). New Haven, Conn., Yale University Press, 1981. A leading and justly acclaimed study of Iran's revolution.

Limbert, John W., *Iran: At War with History*. Boulder, Colo., Westview Press, 1987. A very fine objective history of Iran by a scholar, diplomat, and former hostage.

Ramazani, R. K., *Revolutionary Iran: Challenge and Response in the Middle East*. Baltimore, Md., The Johns Hopkins University Press, 1987. An excellent study of Iranian politics and foreign relations by the dean of American scholars of Iranian diplomatic and political history.

Rubin, Barry M., *Paved with Good Intentions: The American Experience and Iran*. New York, Oxford University Press, 1980. Published soon after the revolution, this book set the standard for studies of American-Iranian relations.

71

Sick, Gary, *All Fall Down: America's Tragic Encounter with Iran*. New York, Random House, 1985. An insider's valuable view of the Carter Administration's futile efforts to develop a viable foreign policy during the Iranian revolution.